C000015879

LAND WARFARE
Brassey's New Battlefield Weapons Systems and
Technology Series into the 21st Century

Volume 7
• • • • • • • • • • • •

Battlefield Command Systems

LAND WARFARE

Brassey's New Battlefield Weapons Systems and Technology Series into the 21st Century

Editor-in-Chief: Colonel R G Lee OBE, Former Military Director of Studies, Royal Military College of Science, Shrivenham, UK

The success of the first and second series on Battlefield Weapons Systems and Technology and the pace of advances in military technology have prompted Brassey's to produce a new Land Warfare series. This series updates subjects covered in the original series and also covers completely new areas. The new books are written for military personnel who wish to advance their professional knowledge. In addition, they are intended to aid anyone who is interested in the design, development and production of military equipment.

Battlefield Command Systems

M.J. Ryan

Australian Defence Force Academy, Canberra, Australia

BRASSEY'S

London

To my father, who encouraged a small boy to wonder why

Copyright © 2000 M J Ryan

All Rights Reserved. No part of this publication may be reproduced, stored in a retrieval system or transmitted in any form or by any means; electronic, electrostatic, magnetic tape, mechanical, photocopying, recording or otherwise, without permission in writing from the publishers.

First English Edition 2000

UK editorial offices: Brassey's, 9 Blenheim Court, Brewery Road, London N7 9NT

A member of the Chrysalis Group plc

UK orders: Littlehampton Books, 10 – 14 Eldon Way, Lineside Estate,

Littlehampton BN17 7HE

North American orders: Books International, PO Box 960, Herndon, VA 20172, USA

M J Ryan has asserted his moral right to be identified as the author of this work.

Library of Congress Cataloging in Publication Data available

British Library Cataloguing in Publication Data

A catalogue record for this book is available from the British Library

ISBN 1 85753 289 9 Hardcover

Cover photograph courtesy of British Aerospace Defence Systems

Typeset by Hedgehog, Upton upon Severn, Worcestershire

Printed by Redwood Books, Trowbridge, Wiltshire

Contents

Foreword

The number and sophistication of battlefield sensors and the capacity of communications systems have increased dramatically since World War Two. The subsequent expansion in data collection and reporting capability has led to a large increase in the volume of information received by a commander and staff. At the same time, however, the pace of modern battle has meant the time available for decision making has correspondingly decreased. The disparity between the vast amount of information received and the time available to process it, cannot be reduced by simply expanding the size of the processing staff. The only solution lies in the extensive application of automation to process large volumes of information and to prepare and disseminate plans within a realistic timeframe. Most modern command systems are therefore automated to some degree to increase the ability of the staff to handle many detailed and time-consuming tasks. Command systems must provide commanders with accurate, timely information that is presented in an appropriate, digestible form.

Of all of the areas of battlefield technology, the study of battlefield command systems must surely be the most complex, not only because of the wide range of underlying technologies and the differences in national emphasis and deployment, but also because of the plethora of variations in terminology. It is therefore not possible to address in a single short book all of the issues in the detail that may be warranted. However, this book does cover the major issues to act as a primer for readers wishing to expand their knowledge in this critical area.

By way of introduction, Chapter 1 provides a brief discussion of command and control on the modern battlefield. Some familiarity with military tactics, doctrine and procedures is assumed.

Chapters 2 to 5 address the technologies that underpin the communications and information systems that support battlefield command systems. Once again, space restrictions constrain the scope of the chapters. However, the major issues are discussed.

Readers familiar with the underlying technologies may skip to Chapters 6 and 7, which build on the previous chapters to provide an overview of tactical communications systems and battlefield information systems.

Michael Ryan
Canberra 2000

1.
Command and Control

INTRODUCTION

Since modern warfare depends on tempo, lethality and survivability, a commander and staff must be supported by an agile, responsive planning process. They also need to cope with the influx of huge amounts of information from intelligence and surveillance systems, both tactical and strategic. In recent conflicts, this has overloaded tactical communications systems as well as the manpower-intensive intelligence process and made it extremely difficult for the commander to process and analyse information in a timely manner.

The success of a commander depends on the timely receipt of accurate information that can be digested readily to allow the preparation of appropriate plans. Of course the mere preparation of a good plan is not sufficient; the plan must be communicated to those who will implement it, and its execution must be controlled. These are the functions of *command and control*, which, on the modern battlefield, have become increasingly dependent on reliable communications and effective information systems.

This chapter introduces the terminology of command and control (C2) and provides an overview of the C2 Cycle. It then briefly describes the heavy reliance that command systems have on the electromagnetic spectrum, and introduces the concept of Information Warfare.

TERMINOLOGY

Perhaps more than in any other field of military endeavour, the topic of command and control has spawned many variations in terminology, for example: command and control (C2); command, control and communications (C3); command, control, communications and computers (C4); communications and information systems (CIS); command, control, communications and intelligence (C3I), command, control, communications, computers and intelligence (C4I), or the latest from the US is C4ISR meaning command, control, communications, computers, intelligence, surveillance and reconnaissance. Most of these alternative terms place additional emphasis on particular parts of the C2 Cycle. However, the drive to become all-inclusive tends to lead to unwieldy terminology. Rather than become too caught up in semantics, we will focus on the C2 Cycle and consider all of the systems that support it under the generic term - *command systems*.

The subject of command and control is far too broad to be treated completely here. Therefore, we will concentrate on the technologies and systems involved in supporting command and control and gaining control of the electronic battlefield. For these purposes then, we will settle for the following working descriptions.

Command

Command is perhaps best described as *the authority vested in an individual for the direction, co-ordination and control of military forces*.

Control

Control is *the means by which command is exercised*. At lower levels, the commander will do much of the controlling. At higher formations, most of the control functions are delegated to staff. Control involves: analysis of requirements; allocation of resources; integration of effort; co-ordination; and monitoring, to allow the commander to respond to changes in the tactical situation.

Information

The ability to command and control depends on the receipt of timely, accurate information that is presented in an appropriate format. Any deterioration in the information reaching a headquarters will lead to a commensurate deterioration in the ability to plan and control. Information can be contained in a variety of forms such as orders, reports, returns and messages. Whilst this information has traditionally been passed over voice and telegraph circuits, much is now sent as data. As the number of battlefield information systems grows, database transfers are also beginning to form a major requirement for information exchange.

In subsequent chapters, we will be interested in how battlefield command systems transfer, process and store these forms of information. We will see that the issue is fundamentally one of ensuring that the information, which is stored in *databases*, is transferred and processed within the time frames dictated by the operational environment.

Command Systems

A *command system* comprises a set of automated and manual procedures to support a commander and staff in their implementation of the C2 Cycle. The essential components of a command system are:

• the commander;

- supporting staffs;
- doctrine and procedures;
- reconnaissance and surveillance and target acquisition (STA) systems;
- communication systems; and
- information systems.

Arguably, the most important component is still the human element, comprising an able commander supported by well-drilled staff and appropriate doctrine and procedures. However, technology is essential to provide the automation necessary to transfer, process and store the large volumes of data on the modern battlefield.

The components of a command system are interdependent and no one in particular can reasonably be singled out. However, we will focus on the last two components and address the technologies that are required to provide appropriate battlefield command systems. We must continue to be mindful, however, that technology alone will not win battles. In that regard, it must be remembered that a command system comprises a set of *automated* and *manual* procedures. Sometimes manual procedures are more appropriate and consideration must be given to the implementation of a set of procedures that can survive the destruction of communications and information systems. Therefore, at the very least, manual procedures have a role in providing backup to technology-based solutions.

THE C2 CYCLE

The interdependence of the various elements of a command system is illustrated by the C2 Cycle shown in Figure 1.1.

The C2 Cycle is also called the *Decision Cycle*, the *Decision-Action Cycle*, the *OODA (or OUDA) Loop* (for the elements of observation, orientation (or understanding), decision and action), or the *Boyd Cycle* after the US Air Force Colonel John Boyd who pioneered the concept. In the US, it is sometimes referred to as the *OODR Loop* (for the elements of observation, orientation, decision and reaction).

The essential elements of the Cycle are:

- **STA or** Observation. Whilst the cycle is continuous, it can be considered to start with STA, or *observation*. The commander receives a wide range of information from many sensors and systems such as: ground-surveillance radar, movement sensors, UAVs, reconnaissance patrols, strategic intelligence systems, and so on. Since this information is invariably reported in digital form, the rapid increase in the number of sensors and surveillance systems is predominantly responsible for the explosion in digital transmission requirements on the modern battlefield.

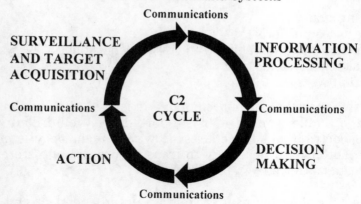

Figure 1.1. The C2 Cycle.

- **Information Processing or *Orientation* or *Understanding*.** The data and information passed to the headquarters must be filtered, processed and then displayed in an appropriate format to be digested by the commander and staff. Automation of this process (and use of artificial intelligence techniques) is essential as the volume of information grows. By the year 2000, it is conservatively estimated that a divisional commander will have available something in the order of 1,000 times the information that would have been available in 1980.

- **Decision Making.** The commander then makes a number of decisions and finalises a plan. We will discuss support for this process in more detail in Chapter 7.

- **Action.** This is the business end of command and control, and the C2 Cycle must assist the commander to take effective action based upon a correct appreciation. However, since few plans last longer than H-hour, the cycle must continue and information begins to flow to support the new operation.

- **Communications.** Surveillance data can only reach the commander if effective, survivable communications systems with sufficient capacity are available from sensor systems through to information processing facilities. The rapid growth in sensor and weapon systems means that communications planners are always struggling to provide systems with sufficient capacity. Within a headquarters, high-speed data networks and voice communications must be provided to facilitate the information processing and decision functions. Finally, the commander must be able to convey orders and to monitor and control the action of combat units. Note that communication appears four times in the loop, and is an essential part of the C2 Cycle. Without communications on the modern battlefield, the commander is deaf, dumb and blind.

The key to success on the battlefield is the ability to navigate through the C2 Cycle more quickly than the enemy. Whilst we have acknowledged that the human factor is important, technology plays a major part in reducing the time spent on each element of the process, particularly through the use of robust communications systems with greater capacity; and faster and more robust information processing systems.

THE MODERN BATTLEFIELD

Operational Environment

On the modern battlefield, the operational environment is defined by five major trends:

- continuous action (day and night)
- increased volume, lethality, range and precision of fire;
- greater dispersion of more mobile, faster units;
- smaller, more-effective units, due to better integration of technology; and
- a dichotomy between greater invisibility (due to dispersion and speed) and increased risk of detection (due to larger numbers of more capable battlefield sensors).

These trends will dramatically affect the nature of future operations. Decisive results will be able to be achieved by smaller, widely dispersed units that will be able to acquire targets and generate large volumes of accurate fire at much greater ranges than is currently possible. This will not only change the way armies are organised and trained, but will significantly affect the way they are commanded and controlled. In particular, the modern battlefield will be characterised by the commander's ability to conduct simultaneous actions.

Simultaneous Action

Due to the limited range of primitive weapons and communications systems, early battles were fought on relatively thin battlefronts behind which commanders were generally free to re-deploy their forces. Wars became more two-dimensional as the extended range of artillery began to limit a commander's freedom of movement behind the front lines. The third dimension was added by aerial interdiction. Doctrine for operations in this three-dimensional battle space was developed and refined during the Cold War, including the US AirLand Battle and the NATO Follow-On-Forces Attack (FOFA) doctrine.

However, the ability to operate in three dimensions is not sufficient, since actions are invariably still sequential. That is, plans are generally phased with one phase starting as another is finished. A command system must assist the modern commander in two important aspects: to conduct multiple simul-taneous actions to paralyse the enemy, as well as to move through the C2 cycle to deal with multiple simultaneous threats. This is the concept of *simultaneous action*.

The purpose of simultaneous action is to paralyse the enemy who cannot move through the C2 Cycle fast enough to cope with the multiple threats. The aim is to present the enemy commander with another action before the last threat has been countered. When these threats are continually presented, the enemy commander cannot regain balance or take effective action against any of the previous threats.

The implementation of simultaneous action has two major implications for the C2 Cycle. First, the friendly commander must be able to command and control multiple actions at the same time, remembering that these actions are being conducted by more mobile forces that are more widely dispersed. Second, to prevent an enemy commander employing simultaneous action, the friendly commander must be able to move through the C2 cycle in such a way as to be able to isolate and deal with multiple threats.

As discussed earlier, technology plays a major part in reducing the time spent on each element of the C2 Cycle. The underlying technologies of information systems are expected to advance a thousand-fold in the next twenty years. In fact, the rate of advance is already so great that it has rendered inadequate current procurement and materiel management processes, a fact we will return to later.

The greater demands of the modern battlefield have a number of effects on communications and information systems, which must be more flexible and adaptable. No longer can command systems be designed solely to support corps or even divisional-level operations. The new-world order requires systems that are modular and expandable to support a variety of operations in diverse environments. Additionally, the traditional niches occupied by systems must be expanded. For example, combat net radio must not only perform its traditional role of voice communications for combat forces, but it must also provide an extension to the digital services of the trunk network. However, more of this in later chapters.

Let's continue this introduction to command systems with a brief look at the heavy reliance that such systems have on the electromagnetic spectrum.

DOMINATING THE ELECTROMAGNETIC SPECTRUM

It is evident from the preceding discussion that movement through the C2 Cycle on the modern battlefield depends heavily on the use of the electromagnetic spectrum, whether for STA, passage of information, processing of information, or destruction of enemy forces. Modern war will be fought in a battlespace comprising the physical battlefield and the electromagnetic spectrum. Heavy reliance on use of the spectrum is a vulnerability that must be exploited in enemy command systems, while being protected in own-force systems. The electromagnetic spectrum can be exploited to:

- monitor enemy transmissions to gather intelligence,
- locate the enemy through his transmissions,
- deceive through the provision of a false electromagnetic picture of the disposition of friendly forces, and
- blind enemy surveillance and target acquisition assets to prevent his acquisition of intelligence.

The C2 Cycle depends very heavily on the electromagnetic spectrum to maximise the effectiveness of STA, communications and information systems. If these are destroyed, degraded or deceived, the C2 Cycle will not operate correctly and the commander and staff will not be able to prosecute war adequately. This has led to the development of the concept of Information Warfare.

Information Warfare

The destruction of Iraqi C2 systems played an important part in the Coalition's success in the Gulf Conflict. Iraqi operations were seriously disrupted and their ability to assess and respond to Coalition actions was severely degraded. The concept of an integrated attack on C2 was based on the US doctrine of Command, Control and Communications Counter Measures (C3CM), which has developed into Information Warfare, which can be defined as:

The integrated use of all military capabilities including destruction, electronic warfare (EW), military deception, psychological operations (PSYOPS) and operational security (OPSEC) supported by all-source intelligence and command systems to deny information to, exploit, degrade, confuse or destroy enemy C2 capabilities and to protect friendly C2, intelligence and command systems against such actions.

There are many other definitions; each nation, and indeed each service, currently tends to have its own. Effectively, however, each definition has the same components and all have the same intent.

We do not have space here for a detailed discussion of Information Warfare. The above definition discusses the military capabilities of physical destruction, EW, deception, PSYOPS and OPSEC. Again, we will concentrate on that component that is most affected by technology, that is EW, which is discussed in some depth in Chapter 6. However, Figure 1.2 briefly illustrates the wide-ranging effects that EW can have on the C2 Cycle.

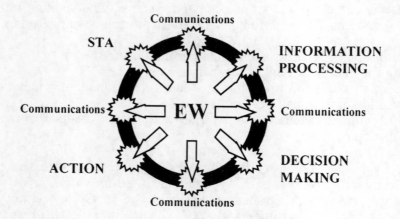

Figure 1.2. EW effect on the C2 Cycle.

EW has the potential to attack any part of the C2 Cycle that depends on the electromagnetic spectrum, including sensors, communications and information systems. In short, on the modern battlefield, denying the enemy use of the electromagnetic spectrum means effectively denying the ability to command and control (certainly in a timely fashion). At the very least, the reduction in the flow of information and speed of decision making will dramatically slow the tempo of operations. 'Own the spectrum' might sound a little trite, but it is a dictum that modern commanders ignore at their peril.

SUMMARY

That concludes our brief introduction to command and control. The simple intention has been to cover basic issues. More detailed discussion is available in another volume in this series and in current writings on doctrine, such as the US TRADOC Pamphlet 525-5 - 'Force XXI Operations'. The remaining chapters address the fundamental technologies underlying communications, information and networking systems and then go on to discuss the issues associated with the provision of communication and information systems on the modern battlefield.

2.
Communications Fundamentals

Communication can be defined as the exchange of information. Humans exchange information in one of three forms: *verbal* (speech); *written* (text) or *visual* (images or video). When the recipient is beyond the range of normal human communication, we must enlist the aid of a *communication system*. As shown in Figure 2.1, a communication system conveys information from originator to recipient (*source* to *sink*) through transmission of electrical signals.

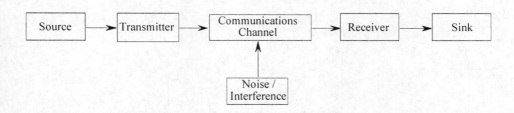

Figure 2.1. A simple communication system.

The *source* converts the original voice, text or image message into an electrical signal. Voice is converted through a microphone; text through a teletypewriter or computer; and images through a camera or video camera. The *transmitter* prepares signals for transmission through amplification, coding and modulation. The *channel* is the medium between transmitter and receiver. It can be a cable, or a radio or light wave. Signals transmitted across the channel can be mixed with other unwanted signals from a variety of sources. Unwanted signals from natural sources are called *noise*; those from man-made sources are called *interference*.

The *receiver* extracts the signal from the channel and passes it on to the *sink*, which converts the electrical signal back into the form of the original message. For voice, the sink will be a speaker; for text, a teletypewriter or a computer; and a television will be used to display video signals.

FUNDAMENTALS OF ANALOGUE SIGNALS

The electrical signals used in communications systems are often complex and difficult to analyse. Fortunately, however, all signals can be considered to be a combination of simple basic building blocks that can be analysed.

Battlefield Command Systems

The following sections assume a basic knowledge of voltage, current and power. Those readers who may not be that familiar with these concepts can refer to Appendix I. Appendix II contains a description of the measurement of decibels (dB).

The Sine Wave

The basic building block we will use for signal analysis is the *sine wave*. The *sine function* (abbreviated as *sin*) is defined as $\sin(\theta)$=opposite/hypotenuse, where θ is the angle between the adjacent side and the hypotenuse of a right-angle triangle.

If θ is measured in degrees, $\sin(\theta)$ will range from 0° to 360° (from a straight line through to a full circle). Figure 2.2 shows how the sine function varies with the angle θ, where θ is in degrees or in radians, where there are 2π radians in a circle (that is, in 360°), so that $\pi/4$=45°, $\pi/2$=90°, π=180°, 2π=360° and so on.

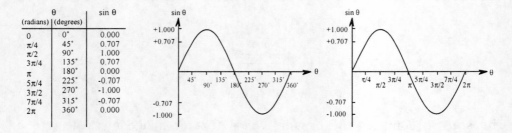

θ (radians)	θ (degrees)	sin θ
0	0°	0.000
π/4	45°	0.707
π/2	90°	1.000
3π/4	135°	0.707
π	180°	0.000
5π/4	225°	-0.707
3π/2	270°	-1.000
7π/4	315°	-0.707
2π	360°	0.000

Figure 2.2. Variation of sine with θ (in degrees and radians).

There are two ways we can use this sinusoidal function to portray an electrical signal. We can compare the instantaneous amplitude of the signal against either the distance it has travelled (Figure 2.3(a)), or the length of time it has been travelling (Figure 2.3(b)).

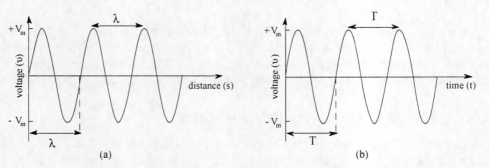

Figure 2.3. The sine wave as a function of (a) distance and (b) time.

The Distance Model

A reasonable analogy of the distance model would be the view you would have of the wave motion of the sea by standing on a cliff top. The equation describing this relationship is:

$$\upsilon(s) = V_m \sin(s)$$

where $\upsilon(s)$ - the signal voltage at a particular point in space;
          V_m - the peak (maximum) value of the signal; and
          s - the distance travelled.

The distance model helps us understand an important property of the wave, which is its *wavelength*, λ. As illustrated in Figure 2.3(a), λ is best measured between peaks of the propagating waveform.

The Time-varying Model

Most often, we want to consider the signal as a time-varying function since it is generally the time variance in the signal that conveys the information. To continue our nautical analogy, this is the view we would have if we were floating in a small boat and could measure our relative height over time as we bobbed up and down. Mathematically, the time-varying relationship is:

$$\upsilon(t) = V_m \sin(\omega t)$$

where $\upsilon(t)$ - the instantaneous signal voltage;
        V_m - the maximum value of the signal voltage; and
        ω - the angular frequency of the signal (defined shortly).

As illustrated in Figure 2.3(b), an important property of the wave is the *period*, T, which is the amount of time after which the waveform repeats itself. Another important property is the *frequency*; that is, the number of cycles (or periods) per second. Frequency, f, is measured in Hertz (Hz) and is defined as $f = 1/T$. As shown in Figure 2.4, a high frequency wave has more cycles per second than a low frequency wave.

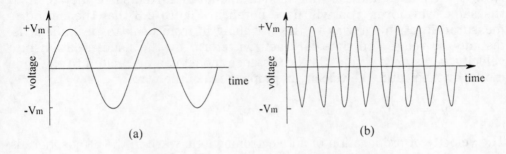

Figure 2.4. A (a) low frequency, and (b) high frequency wave.

Battlefield Command Systems

Angular frequency (ω), is best described pictorially. Figure 2.5 shows how a sinusoidal wave is generated by a rotating phasor of magnitude V_m. At time t=0, the phasor lies on the x-axis and begins to rotate at the velocity of ω radians per second in the anti-clockwise direction. The vertical projection of the rotating phasor generates a sinusoid when plotted against time. The angle of the phasor at any time t is ωt. One complete rotation of the phasor completes 2π radians (or 360°) which generates one complete period of the sinusoid. The time taken to complete the period is therefore 2π/ω.

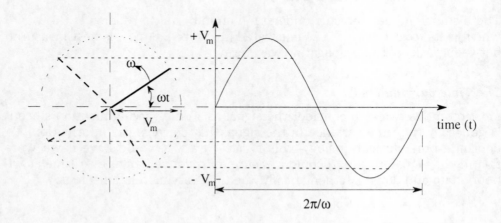

Figure 2.5. Sinusoidal generation by a rotating phasor.

Angular frequency (ω) is related to the period (T):

$$T = \frac{2\pi}{\omega} \qquad \text{or} \qquad \omega = \frac{2\pi}{T} \qquad \text{or} \qquad \omega = 2\pi f$$

The Relationship Between the Models

Now, the distance and the time models should be linked since they refer to the same waveform. You will have noted in Figure 2.3 that the period is measured in a similar way to the wavelength, from peak to peak. That is, distance is related to time for each waveform by the usual relationship: velocity = distance / time. So the distance model can be related to the time model by their ratio, the velocity of propagation of the wave, v_p:

$$v_p = \lambda / T \qquad \text{or} \qquad \lambda = v_p T$$

The velocity of propagation of an electromagnetic wave in the atmosphere is the speed of light, c, which equals 3×10^8 ms^{-1}. Therefore:

$$c = \lambda / T \quad \text{or} \quad \lambda = cT \quad \text{or} \quad \lambda = c/f \quad \text{or} \quad f = c/\lambda$$

Complex Waveforms

Now, we rarely want to pass simple signals across a communications system. Fortunately, however, we can consider complex waveforms to be combinations of simple sine waves. Figure 2.6 shows an example of a complex waveform that can be considered to be the sum of three sine waves at frequencies of 40kHz, 50kHz and 60kHz.

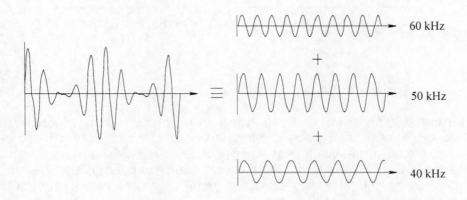

Figure 2.6. A complex waveform expressed as a sum of sine waves.

The Frequency Domain

The frequency of a travelling wave is one of its significant properties. Therefore, it is often useful to view the waveform in the frequency domain where the frequency is plotted against amplitude. Figure 2.7 shows a sine wave with a period of 1ms (a frequency of 1kHz) in the (a) time and (b) frequency domain.

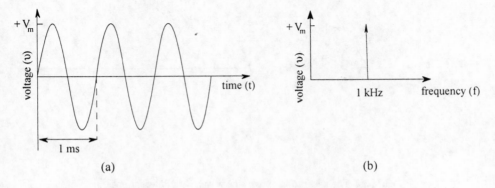

Figure 2.7. A sine wave in the (a) time and (b) frequency domain.

It is difficult to represent complex signals in the time domain. Yet, in the frequency domain, the representation is simply a spike of the appropriate amplitude at the appropriate frequency for each component. For example, Figure 2.8(b) shows the complex waveform in Figure 2.6 in the frequency domain.

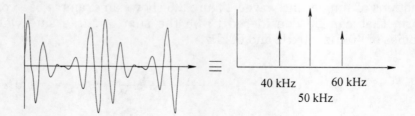

Figure 2.8. A complex waveform in the time and frequency domains.

Bandwidth. This leads us to the measure of *bandwidth,* which is the difference between the highest and lowest frequencies that have to be passed by the system. In the example of Figure 2.8, the bandwidth required to pass the signal is 60kHz-40kHz=20kHz. Apart from simplifying the view of a complex signal, the frequency domain diagram allows the visualisation of the bandwidth required.

Phase

Another important quality of a waveform is its *phase*. Figure 2.9 shows $v_1(t)$, a sine wave generated by a rotating (solid) phasor. A second wave, $v_2(t)$, lags $v_1(t)$ by a phase of θ, and is generated by a (dotted) phasor that is θ radians behind the first. Since the phase reference is arbitrary, phase is relative.

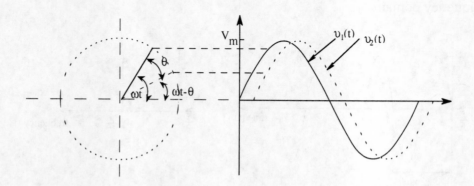

Figure 2.9. The generation of two sine waves with different phases.

Mathematically, the equations describing the waveforms are:

$$\upsilon_1(t) = V_m \sin(\omega t)$$

$$\upsilon_2(t) = V_m \sin(\omega t - \theta)$$

$\upsilon_1(t)$ & $\upsilon_2(t)$ - the instantaneous signal voltages of the two waveforms;
V_m - the peak value of the waveforms;
ω - the angular frequency of each signal; and
θ - the phase of $\upsilon_2(t)$ relative to $\upsilon_1(t)$

We will meet phase a number of times in the following sections and chapters.

Speech Signals

Before leaving the fundamentals of analogue signals, it is instructive to examine the signals produced by the human voice since these are the complex signals that we will often be trying to pass over various types of communications channels. The sounds produced in speech contain frequencies that lie within the range 100Hz to 10,000Hz. The human ear can hear sounds in the range 15Hz to 15,000Hz; that is, the ear can hear far more frequencies than the voice can generate. Most of the energy for speech signals is contained in the lower frequencies, however, and most useful frequencies are contained between about 300Hz and 3,400Hz. Therefore, for speech signals, the bandwidth is 3,400-300=3,100Hz, or 3.1kHz.

The Electromagnetic Spectrum

Due to the size of the electromagnetic spectrum, it is convenient to break it into sections that exhibit common properties as illustrated in Figure 2.10. We are interested in those portions of the spectrum that are suitable for communications; that is, those frequencies in the audible frequency (AF) and radio frequency (RF) ranges.

Audio Frequencies (AF) and Radio Frequencies (RF)

In the AF and RF regions of the spectrum, the International Telecommunication Union (ITU) Radio Regulations define the bands of frequencies outlined in Table 2.1.

Extremely Low Frequency (ELF). The ELF band is not significant in communications due to the extremely small bandwidth available and the enormous antennas required. However, ELF propagation suffers very little attenuation by seawater and therefore has a particular use for communication to submarines.

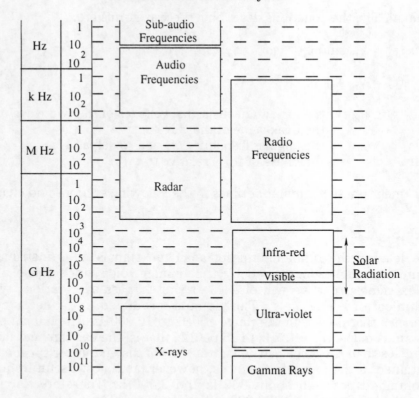

Figure 2.10. The electromagnetic spectrum.

Voice Frequency (VF). VF frequencies are those generated by the voice and able to be received by the ear. Therefore, VF is critical to communications systems, as this frequency range will often be the required input and output of a system.

FREQUENCY	DESIGNATION	WAVELENGTH
30-300 Hz	ELF	10,000-1,000 km
300-3000 Hz	VF	1,000-100 km
3-30 kHz	VLF	100-10 km
30-300 kHz	LF	10-1 km
300-3,000 kHz	MF	1-0.1 km
3-30 MHz	HF	100-10 m
30-300 MHz	VHF	10-1 m
300-3,000 MHz	UHF	1-0.1 m
3-30 GHz	SHF	100-10 mm
30-300 GHz	EHF	10-1 mm

Table 2.1. The AF and RF portions of the electromagnetic spectrum.

Very Low Frequency (VLF) and Low Frequency (LF). VLF and LF suffer the same difficulties as ELF: small bandwidths; and antennas are large and inefficient leading to low radiated powers. However, both bands have similar advantages as ELF for submarine communications but larger bandwidths are available.

Medium Frequencies (MF). The lower MF band is useful for reasonably stable transmission over moderately long distances. This band is commonly used for commercial radio broadcasting as well as fixed services, maritime mobile service, maritime and aeronautical navigation, and amateur communication.

High Frequencies (HF). The HF band provides relatively reliable propagation over long distances with low radiated power. Long-range propagation is principally by skywave and therefore depends on the vagaries of the ionosphere. Surface wave communications over short distances (~50 km) are also possible. The band is used for fixed services, mobile services, amateur transmissions, broadcasting, and maritime mobile service.

Very High Frequency (VHF) and Ultra High Frequency (UHF). Both of these bands can be used for line-of-sight communications, which require the transmission of large bandwidths over short distances. Small, directional antennas are economical and effective. The bands are used for fixed communications services, ground-to-air communications, satellite communications, mobile services, and television.

Super High Frequency (SHF) and Extremely High Frequency (EHF). SHF and EHF are known as the microwave bands and their short wavelengths are propagated by highly directional antennas. Ranges are limited to line-of-sight but long-distance communication can be achieved by radio relay stations. These bands are used for television, satellite communications, and high-speed data services requiring large bandwidths.

Communications Frequencies other than RF and AF. The majority of the communications frequencies are contained within the RF bands. With the advent of optical fibres, however, optical frequencies are also used for communications. More recently, infra-red frequencies are also employed to provide the transmission medium for wireless local area networks.

ANALOGUE MODULATION METHODS

Transmission systems such as cable systems or radio links have sufficient capacity to pass many conversations simultaneously, since the bandwidth required for telephone-quality speech is only 300-3,400Hz. However, these conversations would become interwoven and indistinguishable from each other at the receiver. To avoid this, each signal must be shifted in frequency to a different part of the spectrum.

This translation from one frequency band to another is called *modulation*, where the baseband signal is used to alter the characteristics of a carrier signal at a higher frequency. The three characteristics of the carrier signal that can be altered are the *amplitude*, the *frequency* and the *phase*, leading to: *amplitude modulation*, *frequency modulation* and *phase modulation*.

The general expression for a sinusoidal carrier wave is:

$$\upsilon_c(t) = V_c \sin(\omega_c t + \phi)$$

(2-1)

where $\upsilon_c(t)$ - the instantaneous carrier voltage;
       V_c - the peak value of the carrier voltage;
       ω_c - the angular frequency of the carrier $(2\pi f_c)$; and
       ϕ - the phase of the carrier voltage.

The modulating signal is used to vary one of the properties of the carrier, either the amplitude (V_c), frequency (f_c), or phase (ϕ).

Amplitude Modulation (AM)

Using the sinusoidal carrier of Equation (2-1), ignoring the phase:

$$\upsilon_c(t) = V_c \sin \omega_c t$$

In the simplest case, the modulating signal is also sinusoidal:

$$\upsilon_m(t) = V_m \sin \omega_m t$$

The carrier amplitude will be caused to vary sinusoidally with an angular frequency of ω_m (frequency f_m) about a mean value of V_c volts with a maximum variation of $\pm V_m$ volts. The AM wave is then:

$$\upsilon(t) = (\underbrace{V_c}_{\substack{\text{un modulated} \\ \text{carrier amplitude}}} + \overbrace{\underbrace{V_m \sin \omega_m t}_{\text{variation}}}^{\substack{\text{modulated} \\ \text{carrier amplitude}}}) \sin \omega_c t$$

Figure 2.11(b) shows the resultant waveform where a 1kHz sine wave has amplitude modulated a 10kHz carrier (Figure 2.11(a)). The outline of the wave is known as the *modulation envelope*, which on both sides of the waveform resembles the shape of the modulating signal. The envelope therefore has a maximum amplitude of $|V_c+V_m|$ and a minimum amplitude of $|V_c-V_m|$.

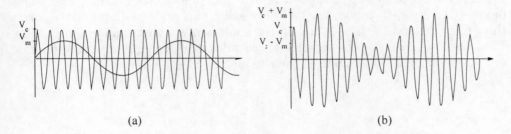

(a)   (b)

Figure 2.11. Carrier and signal and AM modulated waveform.

Expanding, Equation (3-5) becomes:

$$\upsilon(t) = V_c \sin\omega_c t + \frac{V_m}{2}\cos(\omega_c - \omega_m)t - \frac{V_m}{2}\cos(\omega_c + \omega_m)t$$

This expansion is useful because it shows that a sinusoidally modulated carrier wave contains components at three different frequencies: the original carrier frequency (f_c); a lower sidefrequency (f_c-f_m); and an upper sidefrequency (f_c+f_m). It is important to note that the modulating frequency f_m is not present in the modulated waveform.

Figure 2.12 shows the frequency domain representation of a carrier frequency f_c modulated by a single sine wave of frequency f_m. The original frequency f_m (dotted line) is translated by the modulation process to become two sidefrequencies around the carrier, each of which is half the size of the original.

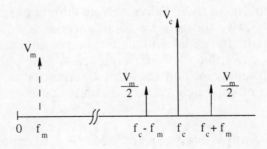

Figure 2.12. AM where a carrier is modulated by a single tone.

As noted earlier, whilst the modulating signal waveform is rarely sinusoidal, it can be viewed as the sum of a number of sinusoids; each of which produces

upper and lower sidefrequencies in the modulated wave, and the modulation
envelope has the same shape as the modulating waveform. As shown in
Figure 2.13, instead of a single sidefrequency, a band of frequencies (in
sidefrequency pairs) is produced above and below the carrier. The band
below the carrier is known as the *lower sideband* and the band above forms
the *upper sideband*. Sidebands are normally drawn with shaped amplitude.
This does not indicate the relative amplitudes of the frequency components,
but simply shows the location of the carrier.

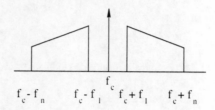

Figure 2.13. The frequency spectrum of an AM waveform.

Modulation Factor

For AM systems, a *modulation factor (m)* is defined:

$$m = \frac{V_m}{V_c}$$

The maximum value is m=1 since this gives a minimum value of zero to the
envelope. If a larger value is used, the waveform will contain a number of
unwanted frequency components extending beyond $f_c \pm f_m$ and the envelope
will no longer resemble the modulating waveform. For telephone quality
speech, m is set to about 0.5.

Power Contained in an AM Wave. Even under maximum modulation
conditions with m=1, two thirds of the total power is developed in the carrier
and only one third in the sidefrequencies. Lower modulation factors will
develop even less power in the sidefrequencies. Since the information is
carried in the sidefrequencies and the same information is contained in each
sideband, full AM is very inefficient and variations that are more efficient have
been developed.

Double-sideband Suppressed-carrier AM. The carrier in an AM wave
transmits no information and represents wasted power. It makes sense,
therefore, to transmit only the sidebands without the carrier, called *double-
sideband suppressed-carrier* (DSBSC) or, more commonly, DSB, as shown
in Figure 2.14(a).

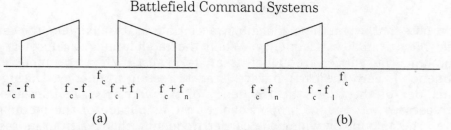

$$f_c$$

$f_c - f_n$ $f_c - f_1$ $f_c + f_1$ $f_c + f_n$ $f_c - f_n$ $f_c - f_1$ f_c

(a)   (b)

Figure 2.14. Frequency spectra of (a) DSB and (b) LSB waveforms.

Single-sideband Suppressed-carrier AM. DSB is still inefficient since the two sidebands are redundant (they carry the same information) and transmission bandwidth must be twice that of the message bandwidth. When only one sideband is transmitted, the transmission is called *single-sideband suppressed carrier (SSBSC)* or more commonly *SSB*, either *upper side band (USB)* or *lower sideband (LSB)*, as shown in Figure 2.14(b). SSB halves the bandwidth of the modulated wave to be equal to that of the baseband signal. All the transmitted power then goes towards transmitting the information. Although always bandwidth efficient, SSB operation has the disadvantage that the transmitters and receivers are more complex and therefore more costly.

Frequency Modulation (FM)

The distinct disadvantage of any form of AM is that any noise will be additive and appear as additional modulation on the carrier. This noise is impossible to remove and will be demodulated as if it was part of the original modulating signal. In FM, the carrier's amplitude remains constant but its frequency is varied by the modulating signal. Any noise added to the carrier during transmission will therefore not affect the information contained in the frequency variations. This gives FM a number of advantages over AM, despite a wider bandwidth requirement.

Figure 2.15 illustrates the frequency modulation of a sinusoidal carrier (solid line) by a sinusoidal signal (dotted line) so that its instantaneous frequency will vary sinusoidally.

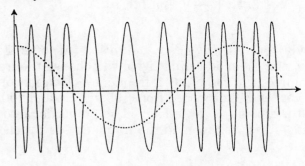

Figure 2.15. An FM wave (sinusoidal modulation superimposed).

First, note that, when the modulating waveform is at its maximum, the carrier wave has its highest frequency. When the modulating waveform is at a minimum, the carrier frequency is at its lowest. When the modulating frequency is zero the carrier wave is at its resting frequency. During the remainder of the time, the frequency of the carrier wave increases or decreases by an amount proportional to the amplitude of the modulating wave. The amount by which the carrier frequency changes from its resting frequency is called the *frequency deviation*, which we will define later. In summary, the carrier frequency is affected by the properties of the modulating waveform in the following way: *amplitude* – determines how far the carrier shifts from its resting frequency; *polarity* – determines the direction of the shift; and *frequency* – dictates the rate of the shift.

If f is the carrier frequency at any time, the unmodulated carrier is:

$$\upsilon_c(t) = V_c \cos 2\pi ft$$

(2-2)

The modulating sinusoidal signal is described as:

$$\upsilon_m(t) = V_m \cos 2\pi f_m t$$

The modulated carrier will vary around a resting frequency f_c so that:

$$f = f_c + f_\Delta V_m \cos 2\pi f_m t$$

(2-3)

where f_Δ is called the *frequency-deviation constant*.

Substituting Equation (2-3) into Equation (2-2) gives:

$$\upsilon(t) = V_c \cos[2\pi(f_c + f_\Delta V_m \cos 2\pi f_m t)t]$$

which, after some calculus, can be written in the more useful format:

$$\upsilon(t) = V_c \cos\left(2\pi f_c t + \frac{f_\Delta}{f_m} V_m \sin 2\pi f_m t\right)$$

Frequency Deviation. The *frequency deviation* (Δf) of an FM waveform is the amount by which the modulating signal will change the frequency of the carrier. For example, if a radio has a frequency deviation of $\Delta f = \pm 50Hz$, then a 200MHz carrier will be varied from 199.95MHz and 200.05MHz. From Equation (2-3), the amount of deviation will be proportional to the amplitude of the modulating signal voltage and the frequency-deviation constant such that:

$$\Delta f = f_\Delta V_m$$

There is no maximum value to the frequency deviation that can be obtained in a FM system (as opposed to AM where the maximum amplitude variation corresponds to m=1). For any given system, however, a maximum allowable frequency deviation, the *rated system deviation* Δf_{max}, must be specified since the FM bandwidth increases with the increase in frequency deviation and each system must have a defined bandwidth limitation. Since frequency deviation is directly proportional to the modulating signal voltage, Δf_{max} defines the maximum allowable modulating signal voltage.

Modulation Index. The FM modulation index (m_f or β) is the ratio of the frequency deviation of the carrier to the modulating frequency. m_f is measured in radians and determines the amplitudes of the frequency components of the modulated wave.

$$m_f = \frac{\Delta f}{f_m}$$

Deviation Ratio. m_f varies as the frequency of the modulating signal changes. This is not useful to use as a design constraint, so the *deviation ratio, D,* is defined as the value of the modulation index when both the frequency deviation and the modulating frequency are at their maximum. Military radio sets use a low value of D (between 1 and 2) to economise on bandwidth.

$$D = \frac{\Delta f_{max}}{f_{m(max)}}$$

Frequency Spectrum of an FM Wave

The amplitudes of the FM carrier and sidefrequencies depend on the value of the modulation index, as tabulated in Table 2.2.

m_f	Carrier	1	2	3	4	5	6	7	8	9
0.00	1.00									
0.25	0.98	0.12								
0.50	0.94	0.24	0.03							
1.00	0.77	0.44	0.11	0.02						
1.50	0.51	0.56	0.23	0.06	0.01					
2.00	0.22	0.58	0.35	0.13	0.03					
2.50	-0.05	0.50	0.45	0.22	0.07	0.02				
3.00	-0.26	0.34	0.49	0.31	0.13	0.04	0.01			
4.00	-0.40	-0.07	0.36	0.43	0.28	0.13	0.05	0.02		
5.00	-0.18	-0.33	0.05	0.36	0.39	0.26	0.13	0.05	0.02	
6.00	0.15	-0.28	-0.24	0.11	0.36	0.36	0.25	0.13	0.06	0.02
7.00	0.30	0.00	-0.30	-0.17	0.16	0.35	0.34	0.23	0.13	0.06
8.00	0.17	0.23	-0.11	-0.29	-0.10	0.19	0.34	0.32	0.22	0.13
9.00	-0.09	0.24	0.14	-0.18	-0.27	-0.06	0.20	0.33	0.30	0.21
10.00	-0.25	0.04	0.25	0.06	-0.22	-0.23	-0.01	0.22	0.31	0.29

Table 2.2. FM spectral components (amplitude relative to the carrier).

Example. Plot the frequency spectrum of an FM wave, $m_f = 2$.

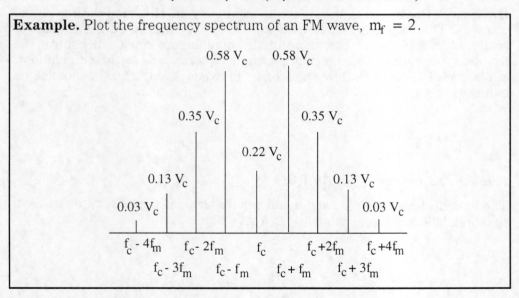

Bandwidth. The extent of the FM spectrum is potentially infinite regardless of whether the baseband is band-limited. However, practical FM systems rely on the fact that, sufficiently far away from the carrier, the spectral components are small and may be discarded without causing distortion. On this assumption, the bandwidth required for an FM wave is given by Carson's rule, which is valid for $D \leq 2$:

$$BW = 2(\Delta f + f_{m(max)})$$

Power contained in an FM wave. Since the amplitude of an FM wave does not vary, the total power contained in the wave is constant and equal to the unmodulated carrier power.

FM Capture Effect. An FM receiver has the ability (called the *capture effect*) to suppress the weaker of two signals at or near the same frequency. In AM, both signals would be heard at the receiver, as the demodulated effect would be the addition of both audio signals. In FM, only the stronger signal will be heard, which has the advantage of ignoring any interference at or near the same frequency. Whilst the capture effect is an attractive feature, it has a significant disadvantage when the wanted signal is weaker than a strong interfering or jamming signal. This effect would not occur in AM systems where both signals would be heard in relative strengths. An AM receiver therefore has the ability to continue to work through lower levels of interference and gracefully degrade as the level of interference is increased. On the other hand, the FM receiver will remain interference-free and then suddenly be captured when the interference signal has reached the necessary power level.

In addition, FM is more efficient than AM and is much less susceptible to noise and interference. The main disadvantage of FM is, of course, the much wider bandwidth required (perhaps 7 to 15 times wider than SSB). Since FM requires a wider bandwidth, higher frequencies must be used, at which reception is generally limited to line-of-sight. FM modulation and demodulation equipment is more complex and expensive. The capture effect may also be a disadvantage when a receiver is near the edge of the service area and it may be captured by an unwanted signal.

Phase Modulation (PM)

PM is very similar to FM except that, instead of the frequency, the instantaneous phase of the carrier is varied at a rate proportional to the modulating frequency and by an amount equal to the amplitude of the modulating signal. Again, the carrier amplitude remains unaltered. PM is rarely used in practice, so we will not consider it any further here.

FUNDAMENTALS OF DIGITAL SIGNALS

In modern communications systems analogue information is often converted into a digital form since digital signals have a number of significant advantages. We will discuss each of these later, but briefly they are:

- all digital signals have the same form ('ones' or 'zeros');

- easier storage;
- easier switching;
- lower susceptibility to noise and more easily regenerated;
- if a communication system is all digital only one type of circuitry is required;
- signals can be more easily multiplexed to share the same channel;
- encryption is more easily implemented; and
- error correction and detection is easier.

It must be noted that digital signals require greater bandwidth and the signals are more complex. However, the benefits significantly outweigh the disadvantages.

Digital signals require some coding or quantisation of an analogue signal to a limited number of discrete values, each of which can be identified by a digit as one element of the code. The codes most commonly used are binary codes and the element of the code is called a _binary digit_ (bit), which can take one of two values: 0 or 1. The states of the symbol can be represented by voltage levels, such as ±5V, as illustrated in Figure 2.16.

There are two ways to transmit digital signals. In *baseband* transmission, voltage levels are transmitted directly. Alternatively, as addressed in the next section, digital signals can be used to modulate an analogue carrier for transmission over longer distances. First, baseband digital signals.

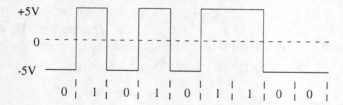

Figure 2.16. A digital signal.

Baseband Digital Signals

Digital signals are less susceptible to noise than their analogue counterparts, where the information is contained in the small variations in the signal amplitude. Attenuation in the channel and the addition of noise tend to distort the signal so that some of the original information is lost, often irretrievably. The information in digital signals is contained in the gross value of each bit, not in the small variations of the signal. As the bit is attenuated and noise is added, the information content remains unchanged until the bit can no longer be distinguished as its original value. Therefore, as long as a '1' can be distinguished from a '0' and vice versa, the information has not been lost.

The advantage of digital signals is that they can be regenerated. Figure 2.17 shows how an original signal (Figure 2.17(a)) is attenuated and noise-affected (Figure 2.17(b)). Provided that the bits can still be identified, the original signal can be perfectly regenerated (Figure 2.17(c)). Therefore, digital signals can generally be re-generated as often as required, without the unwanted amplification of noise. After each re-generation, the digital signal is a precise copy of the original; whereas after analogue amplification, the analogue signal is stronger, but noisier.

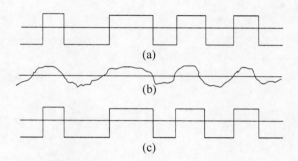

(a)

(b)

(c)

Figure 2.17. Regeneration of a digital signal.

Signalling Speed

The speed at which digital signals can be sent is called the *signalling speed*, which can be the source of considerable confusion. It is important to note the distinction between the signalling speed measurements of *Baud rate* and *bit rate* (or *data transmission rate*). Baud rate is a measurement of the number of **symbols** transmitted per second, whilst bit rate refers to the number of **bits** per second (bps). Obviously if there is one bit allocated to each symbol, the bit rate and the Baud rate will be the same. Normally, however, we can allocate more than one bit to each symbol. If, for example, three bits per symbol were allocated then the bit rate would be three times the Baud rate.

Signalling speed is limited by the available bandwidth, and by the noise in the channel. The available bandwidth affects the baseband signalling rate such that the baseband signalling speed is limited to twice the system bandwidth. For example, a 3kHz channel could accommodate a 6kbps digital signal. Remember this is the baseband signalling speed. Later we will discuss the bandwidth required to pass the digital signals over a radio carrier.

Asynchronous / Synchronous Transmission

Data transmission can be either *asynchronous* or *synchronous* as illustrated in Figure 2.18. Asynchronous transmission occurs without significant prior coordination between the source and the sink. Each block of data is sent by the source, which receives warning of each block by a start bit and notification of the end of the block with a stop bit. Synchronous transmission relies on both the source and sink running oscillators that are continually synchronised so that only a few coordinating (synchronisation) pulses are contained in each block of data. Generally, synchronous transmission is used for data rates of more than 1,200bps (excluding the networking techniques discussed in Chapter 4).

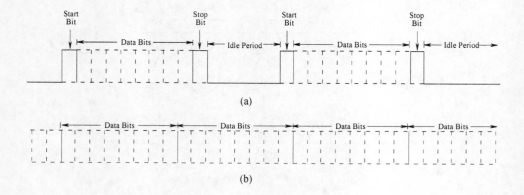

(a)

(b)

Figure 2.18. (a) Asynchronous and (b) synchronous transmission.

DIGITISATION OF ANALOGUE SIGNALS

Analogue signals are converted to digital signals through a process of *waveform coding*, *source coding* or some combination of both. In waveform coding, the amplitude of the waveform is coded without using any knowledge of the waveform. In source coding, the waveform is modelled and selected features of the model are sent to the receiver, which uses these features to recreate the waveform.

Waveform Coding Techniques

Sampling

The first step in analogue to digital conversion is the voltage sampling of the analogue signal. The original signal must be sampled at a rate (f_s) that is at least twice the highest frequency (f_{max}) present in the analogue signal being sampled, so that $f_s \geq 2f_{max}$. At this sampling rate, called the *Nyquist rate*, the samples provide sufficient information to reconstruct the original waveform.

Pulse-code Modulation

In *pulse-code modulation (PCM)* the analogue signals are first sampled and then encoded into a binary code that is transmitted as a digital stream. At the receiver, these PCM codes are decoded into pulses that are then used to reconstruct the analogue waveform. The encoder converts a series of analogue voltages into a digital stream. To understand how it does this, we need a brief revision of binary algebra. Table 2.3 shows how voltage levels from 0V to 7V can be allocated three-bit binary numbers. With three bits in a binary system, the number of levels that can be represented is $2^3=8$, with four bits, $2^4=16$ could be represented, and so on.

Voltage Level	Binary Code
0	000
1	001
2	010
3	011
4	100
5	101
6	110
7	111

Table 2.3. Conversion of eight voltage levels to three-bit binary code.

The waveforms generated by the PCM coding system are illustrated in Figure 2.19. At time t1 the analogue signal has a voltage of 4.25V, which corresponds to the closest binary code of 100, at time t2 the appropriate code is 110 and so on.

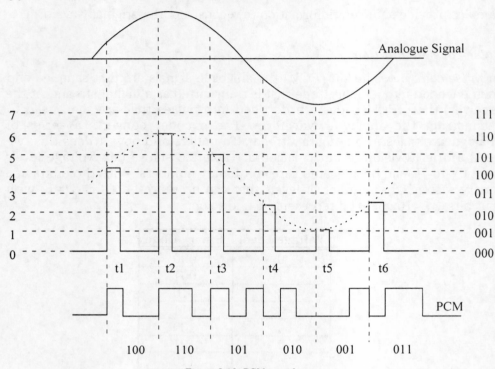

Figure 2.19. PCM waveforms.

With only eight levels in Figure 2.19, the precise value of the waveform cannot always be represented. For example, at time t1, the analogue voltage we wished to represent was 4.25V but we had to send the nearest level (binary code 100) which the receiver will interpret as an original level of 4V, an error of 0.25V. Limiting the number of voltage levels is called *quantisation*. The error associated with the encoding to a restricted number of levels is therefore called *quantisation error* or *quantisation noise*. The larger the number of levels, the smaller the quantisation error and thence the better quality of the digitisation. From Figure 2.19 you can also note that a signal with better quality would result if the sampling frequency was increased.

Transmission Bit Rate. For digitised voice, the maximum frequency is 3.4kHz and sampling is normally conducted at 8kHz. If an 8-bit coder is used (that is, $2^8=256$ quantising levels) then the channel transmission rate is 8000x8=64kb/s.

Delta Modulation

Delta modulation is an incremental PCM system where, rather than transmitting the absolute amplitude of each sample, only the changes from sample to sample are transmitted. This provides a simpler system and requires less information to be transmitted. Delta-modulation produces a one-element code in which a '1' is transmitted if the current sample is greater than the previous sample and a '0' is transmitted if the sample is lower. The range of signal amplitudes is divided into a similar number of quantisation levels (steps) as in PCM systems. The step size is called Δ hence the name *delta modulation*. An illustration is given in Figure 2.20.

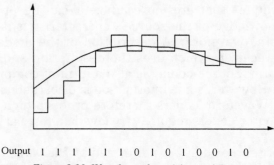

Output 1 1 1 1 1 1 0 1 0 1 0 0 1 0

Figure 2.20. Waveforms for a delta modulator.

Delta modulation systems suffer similar distortions to PCM when the step size is too small (leading to *slope overload*) or too large (*quantisation noise*) or the sampling period is too long (*granular noise*).

Transmission Bit Rate. To transmit digitised voice over a channel, delta modulation only requires one bit per sample. However, to avoid slope overload, it is normal to sample at twice the Nyquist rate (16,000 samples per second for speech). Despite this higher sampling rate, the bit rate required for delta modulation is: 1x16,000=16kbps, which is one quarter of the rate required for PCM. By using the companding techniques described below, systems that are more modern operate as low as 9.6kbps.

In delta modulation, there is only one step, so quantisation noise is large at small signal amplitudes unless small step sizes are also used. However, as we saw above, small step sizes lead to slope overload. It is therefore desirable to have an adaptive technique where the step size is modified according to the signal amplitude. Techniques that address this include *adaptive delta modulation (ADM)*, or more commonly *variable slope delta modulation (VSDM)*.

Delta modulation has a number of advantages over PCM. It requires less bandwidth and has better resistance to noise. Synchronisation is also easier in delta modulation and simpler equipment is required.

Because of these advantages, delta modulation has found wide application in military communications where low-bit-rate digital systems are required. However, delta modulation has a couple of disadvantages in that the quality is generally poorer and there is increased error due to slope overload.

Source Coding Techniques

A waveform coder does not know about the signal being coded and simply codes the signal as it is presented. Relatively large bandwidths are therefore required to achieve the desired quality. When bandwidth is limited, such as at HF, coding techniques that are more efficient can be provided by *source coding*, where knowledge of the source's characteristics is used to create a model of the source waveform. A description of the model's parameters is then sent to the receiver, which uses the description and the model to re-create the waveform. Source coding is also a form of compression, providing reduced bit rates. However, some information is discarded and a lower quality generally results. Waveform coders therefore produce high quality signals at high data rates. Source coders require very low data rates at a lower quality.

A common type of source coding is performed by the *voice coder* or *vocoder*, which removes sufficient redundancy from speech so that the bit rate is reduced to 2.4kbps; low enough for line transmission and narrowband HF.

Line Coding

After source or waveform coding, the digital signal may be transmitted in its original form. Often, however, *line coding* is performed to prepare the signal for transmission by: eliminating DC and lower frequency components to save power; including synchronisation information; providing error detection and correction; and providing some form of encryption. Line coding is provided by a coder/decoder or *codec*, which will often include the waveform or source encoder.

Error Detection and Correction

A critical aspect in data transmission is the determination of whether the received data is error-free. To do this, some form of *error protection*, or *error detection and correction* is utilised. The numbers of errors at the output of the receiver can be reduced by adding additional information to the message to increase the receiver's decision-making ability. This additional redundant information increases the overhead that is included in the transmission.

Once detected, an error must be corrected. There are two main techniques:

- **Automatic Repeat Requests (ARQ).** This is the simplest strategy for the correction of errors. Once an error has been detected, the receiver requests the transmitter to re-transmit the portion of data that was in error. This can be a very powerful mechanism for the correction of errors, but can produce very low data rates in high-noise environments.

- **Forward Error Correction (FEC).** In this method, the receiver is able to correct errors without reference to the transmitter by using additional information transmitted along with the data. The receiver can correct a small number of the errors that have been detected; if it cannot correct all of them, the data must be re-transmitted.

Encryption

An important advantage of digitisation, particularly for military communications, is that the signals can then be encrypted. With analogue signals, only limited security can be implemented through the use of scramblers. On the other hand, sophisticated coding can be achieved for digital signals using *ciphers* or *codes*. The line coding process therefore includes encryption (although the encryption equipment is normally separate from the codec).

DIGITAL MODULATION METHODS

As discussed earlier, data can be transmitted between the source and the sink by directly connecting them with cable and transmitting digital signals directly as baseband DC pulses. For longer ranges, the DC signals must be used to modulate a carrier at either voice frequency (VF) for line transmission or radio frequency (RF) for radio transmission. In that case, there are three modulation methods that are the simplest forms of AM, FM and PM: *amplitude-shift keying (ASK), frequency-shift keying (FSK)* and *phase-shift keying (PSK)* respectively.

ASK is normally implemented by the on-off-keying of a carrier as illustrated in Figure 2.21. ASK is also known as (interrupted) carrier wave (I)CW. CW has been of immense importance in military and civilian communications systems in the past and is normally implemented using Morse code. With the advent of systems with larger bandwidths sufficient for speech and data, the use of CW has reduced significantly. It will remain, however, a very important communication mode particularly in the HF band, due to the considerable advantage offered over all other forms of modulation under the most adverse communications conditions.

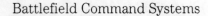

(a)

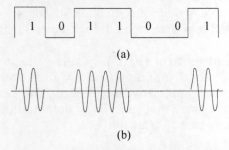

(b)

Figure 2.21. The (a) original digital and (b) ASK waveforms.

ASK, like all AM systems, suffers from significant distortion of the carrier amplitude. It is therefore useful for simple audible codes such as Morse code but has trouble coping with the more complex telegraph codes required to increase the data rate.

FSK

Amplitude distortion can be ignored by using the different voltage levels of the binary digits to displace the carrier above and below the assigned frequency by an amount known as the *shift*. Typical values are narrow shift, 85Hz, and wide shift, 850Hz. As with other forms of FM, the wider shift gives greater noise immunity, whilst the narrow shift will conserve bandwidth. FSK is illustrated in Figure 2.22.

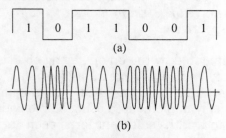

Figure 2.22. The (a) original digital and (b) FSK waveforms.

The form of FSK described above is called *binary* FSK (BFSK), because the shift is between two frequencies. Signalling speed can be increased (at the expense of bandwidth) by extending the number of frequencies to a number M. Such a system is called an *M-ary* FSK system. For example, 4-ary FSK would have half the baud rate of BFSK. BFSK is the predominate means of passing data over analogue radio links since existing analogue FM radios can be used. However, radio links designed specifically for data transmission generally employ PSK.

PSK

PSK is widely used by both military and civilian communications systems. The carrier phase is shifted between two discrete values, normally 0° (logic 1) and 180° (logic 0). In a variation called *differential phase-shift keying (DPSK)*, a phase reversal takes place for each logical '1' whether the symbol before was a logical '0' or a '1'. No phase change occurs at the incidence of a logical '0'. This helps prevent the receiver from confusing a '0' as a '1' and vice versa. Figure 2.23 illustrates PSK and DPSK.

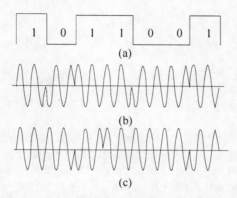

Figure 2.23. The (a) original digital, (b) PSK, and (c) DPSK waveforms.

Further increases in information rate can be achieved within the smaller bandwidth and lower power requirements of PSK. The rate can be doubled by using *four-phase* or *quadrature PSK (QPSK)*, which has phase shifts of 45°, 135°, 225°, and 315° so that two bits of information can be indicated for each phase. Figure 2.24 compares the polar diagram for a QPSK system with a BPSK system.

Hybrid techniques combine ASK with PSK to produce codes represented not only by varying phases, but also by varying amplitudes. Techniques that combine phase and amplitude changes are called Quadrature Amplitude Modulation (QAM). The V.32 (9,600bps) modem standard employs QAM with 45° phase changes with two levels of amplitude, allowing 16 different states to transmit four bits in every symbol.

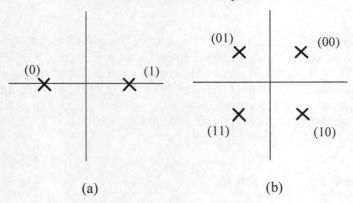

Figure 2.24. Polar diagram for (a) BPSK and (b) QPSK.

Bandwidth

The bandwidth required for digital modulation depends on the baseband bandwidth and the method of modulation. The practical RF bandwidths for the three modulation techniques are: twice the symbol rate for ASK and PSK and three times the symbol rate for FSK. For example, to transmit a 16kbps digital baseband signal, 3x16=48kHz of RF bandwidth is required for FSK and 2x16=32kHz for PSK and ASK. PSK is therefore the preferred technique for digital radios, due to its bandwidth and power efficiency. However, older analogue FM radios naturally use FSK for data transmission.

Modems

The modulation and demodulation of the digital signal to be transmitted over line or radio is conducted by a *modulator/demodulator (modem)*. There are three main types of modem: *baseband*, *VF*, and *RF modem*. Each translates the baseband signal to a different frequency range.

Baseband Modem. A baseband modem performs digital modulation and directly transmits DC pulses to line. Signalling speed and distance are limited by distortion of the pulses. Baseband signals also cannot be transmitted through systems with amplifiers and other devices that only operate with AC signals. In those cases, the baseband signal must be used to modulate a carrier at either VF or RF.

VF Modem. A VF modem performs digital modulation by using the DC pulses to ASK, FSK, or PSK modulate a VF carrier, which allows transmission over existing telephone lines or radio channels that have been designed to accept VF with bandwidths of approximately 3kHz.

RF Modem. If transmission over other types of medium is required, modulation is performed to other frequency ranges. For example, transmission over radio requires the use of an HF, VHF or UHF modem.

MULTIPLEXING TECHNIQUES

Modulation translates the baseband signal to a suitable frequency for a given transmission path. However, it would be very inefficient if only one signal could be sent over each path. *Multiplexing* allows messages from several sources to be transmitted as a complete group of *channels* over a single transmission path using *frequency-division multiplexing (FDM)* or *time-division multiplexing (TDM)*.

FDM

As illustrated in Figure 2.25, FDM systems use SSB modulation to allocate each channel to a certain portion of the available bandwidth.

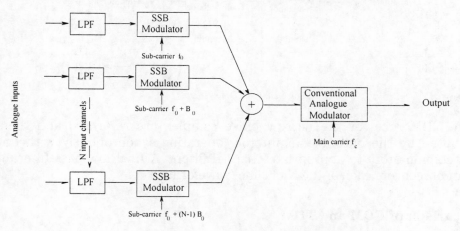

Figure 2.25. An FDM transmitting system.

Each input channel is band-limited by a low-pass filter (LPF) to a maximum frequency, f_m to prevent *crosstalk* from overlapping adjacent channels after modulation. Each channel is modulated onto an appropriate *sub-carrier* to translate the channel to its allotted position. To assist in de-multiplexing, vacant frequency bands called *guard bands, B_g* are placed between channels to assist in channel separation. Each sub-carrier is separated by $B_0 = f_m + B_g$. The FDM signal is then modulated onto the main carrier, f_c, typically by either FM or SSB.

At the receiver, the main carrier is demodulated and each channel of the group separated out by channel filters of bandwidth f_m. Each channel is then demodulated with the appropriate sub-carrier.

TDM

A typical baseband TDM system is illustrated by Figure 2.26. The first operation of the TDM system is the sampling process by the input commutator, a device that sequentially samples all N input channels once per revolution. The low-pass filter on each input channel constrains the input spectrum to a maximum frequency f_m so the sampling rate must be at $2f_m$. The input commutator has two tasks: to take a sample of each of the input waveforms and, to interleave sequentially these N pulse samples. This latter function is the TDM operation.

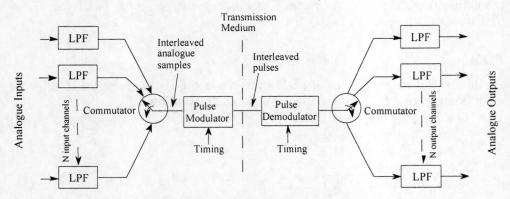

Figure 2.26. A TDM system.

At the TDM receiver the narrow pulse samples are reformed and then distributed by the output commutator (operating synchronously with the input commutator) to appropriate channel filters. A final low-pass filtering operation recovers each of the N channel waveforms.

Comparison of FDM and TDM

Both FDM and TDM concentrate many individual channels into one. However, the transmission path is shared in different ways. FDM channels operate in parallel with each user allocated a portion of the available frequency spectrum for the entire time. In TDM, the entire frequency spectrum is allocated to each user for a portion of time. FDM is more suited to analogue signals; TDM to digital.

TRANSMITTER DESIGN

A transmitter modulates the information from the source onto a carrier and amplifies the result to the required power level for transmission.

AM Transmitters

There are two broad classes of AM transmitter: *low-level* and *high-level*, depending on the power level at which modulation takes place.

Low-level Transmitter. Low-level operation is shown in Figure 2.27. The audio signal is amplified to some extent before modulating the carrier (generated by the local oscillator) but large amplification occurs after modulation. This technique is used by SSB transmitters since it is much easier to do the necessary filtering at low power levels.

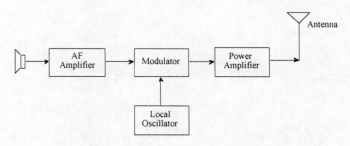

Figure 2.27. Low-level AM transmitter.

High-level Transmitter. Low-level modulation requires substantial linear amplification to reach transmission power levels and it is often better to employ high-level modulation as shown in Figure 2.28. Here, efficient use is made of RF amplifiers for the carrier but high-power AF amplifiers are required. The efficiency of high-level modulation is utilised for DSB sound broadcast and for VHF/UHF mobile transmitters.

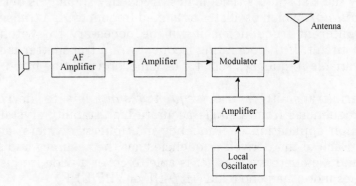

Figure 2.28. High-level AM transmitter.

FM Transmitters

The FM transmitter in Figure 2.29 is similar to the low-level AM transmitter, except for an additional *pre-emphasis network* before the modulator.

The Pre-emphasis Network. The pre-emphasis network is the first half of a system that includes a de-emphasis, network in the receiver. The pre-emphasis/de-emphasis system reduces frequency-modulated noise that affects the signal during transmission. The noise spectrum from an FM detector varies linearly and increases with frequency. The noise therefore affects the high frequencies, the distortion of which dramatically affects intelligibility of the received signal. The pre-emphasis network amplifies the higher-frequency content of the audio signal more than the lower frequencies. The de-emphasis network in the receiver compensates for this by reducing the gain of the higher-frequency audio signal thereby reducing (flattening) the frequency-modulated noise.

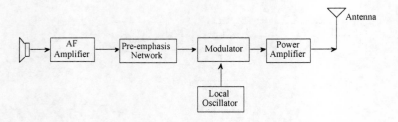

Figure 2.29. FM transmitter.

Local Oscillator (LO)

To allow the receiver to demodulate the signal correctly, a transmitter must generate a stable carrier frequency. In SSB systems, the ability to re-insert the suppressed carrier at the receiver will depend on the stability of the carrier generated by the transmitter. The highest frequency stability is obtained with a *crystal oscillator*, which oscillates at a fixed-frequency. If a transmitter is to operate at different frequencies, it will be necessary to switch different crystals into circuit. If the operating frequency of a transmitter is frequently changed, a variable-frequency oscillator of some kind must be fitted.

Many modern transmitters use *frequency synthesis* to derive all the necessary frequencies from a single accurate high-stability crystal oscillator source through application of frequency multipliers, dividers, adders and subtractors. Each of the derived frequencies has the accuracy and stability of the source and a modern synthesiser is able to cover a wide frequency band, and sometimes more than one band (HF/VHF or VHF/UHF).

RECEIVER DESIGN

The receiver must be able to select the desired signal from all the signals present at the antenna. It must then amplify and demodulate the signal and present it to the source. For long ranges, received signal strengths will be very low and will require considerable amplification. However, too much amplification will reduce the bandwidth of the receiver. The basis of a *superheterodyne* receiver in Figure 2.30 is the conversion of the wanted signal frequency into a constant frequency known as the *intermediate frequency* (IF). It is at the IF that most of the gain and the selectivity of the receiver is provided without affecting the bandwidth of the receiver.

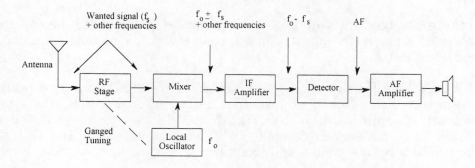

Figure 2.30. AM superheterodyne receiver.

RF Stage. Although the antenna tuning has already restricted incoming frequencies, the RF Stage must perform limited filtering to prevent certain troublesome frequencies. Additionally, the incoming signal is very weak, and is amplified by the RF Stage before being passed to the mixer. The RF Stage:

- efficiently couples antenna to receiver,
- generates little or no noise,
- amplifies (up to 1,000 times) at frequencies above 3MHz,
- must screen the LO from the antenna to prevent the LO frequency from being radiated, and
- pre-selects to remove or avoid a number of troublesome frequencies.

LO. The LO frequency could be higher or lower than the wanted frequency. It is usual to choose the LO to be $f_o = f_s + f_i$, so that the electronics are easier to build. When the RF Stage is tuned to a particular frequency, the LO must be tuned to a frequency equal to the sum of the signal and the IF. Since the IF is fixed, the LO is adjusted so that the correct difference frequency is obtained. It is convenient if the tuning of both these circuits can be carried out by a single control, called *ganging*. The maintenance of the correct frequency difference between the RF Stage and LO frequencies is known as *tracking*.

IF Amplifier. The purpose of the IF Amplifier is to provide most of the gain (typically 100,000 to 10,000,000 times) and the selectivity of the receiver. Since the IF Amplifier operates at a fixed frequency, it can be designed to provide optimum gain and bandwidth characteristics. The choice of IF is a compromise between many, often conflicting, factors. Commercial HF AM broadcast receivers employ an IF bandwidth of 10kHz and an IF of commonly 455kHz, 456kHz or 465kHz. Commercial VHF FM broadcast receivers require an IF bandwidth of about 200kHz, and use an IF that is almost always 10.7MHz. The IF for higher RF frequencies is mostly 70MHz. Often, two or more IFs are used in a *double conversion* receiver to avoid the above compromises.

Detector Stage. The output of the IF Amplifier is applied to the detector where the signal is demodulated in accordance with the modulation scheme used in the radio.

AF Stage. The demodulated signal is amplified by the AF Stage to drive the loudspeaker, handpiece or other output device. After detection, the signal level will be approximately $100\mu W$, which will need to be amplified to 100mW for portable receivers and to 100W for larger receivers. The AF Stage will include a volume control and sometimes treble and bass controls. It may also include a *squelch* or muting facility.

FM Receiver

The receiver of Figure 2.30 is suitable for AM signals. For FM signals, the receiver has a very similar structure except that the different modulation technique requires a different detector circuit. Additionally, as shown in Figure 2.31, an FM receiver has two further circuits: a *limiter* and a *de-emphasis network*.

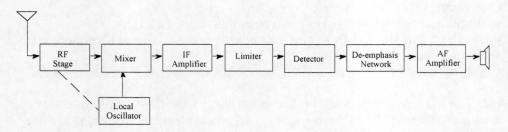

Figure 2.31. FM superheterodyne receiver.

Limiter. Any amplitude variations in the signal are clipped before the detector to avoid distortion during demodulation. This clipping removes any AM noise on the signal but does not affect the information carried by the frequency variations.

The De-emphasis Network. The de-emphasis network is the second half of the pre-emphasis / de-emphasis system described earlier.

TRANSMISSION MEDIA

The term *transmission media* refers to the different types of physical media through which signals will travel. A *transmission line* is a pair of wires, parallel or coaxial, that conveys electrical energy from one point to another. Assume that the transmitter is a simple AC generator, with the output terminals going positive and negative alternatively at frequency f Hz. After turning on, the electrical charges move down the transmission line in the direction shown in Figure 2.32.

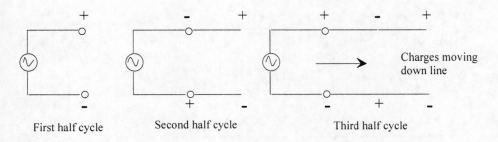

First half cycle   Second half cycle   Third half cycle

Figure 2.32. Movement of charge down a transmission line.

Now, movement of charge equates to current flow, so we can say that we have a wave of alternating current flowing down the transmission line with a peak of I amps, as shown in Figure 2.33. Note that the charges have opposite polarity in each leg of the line.

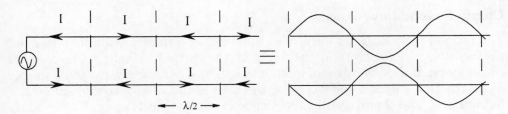

Figure 2.33. Flow of current in a transmission line.

The whole pattern is moving away from the generator with a velocity of propagation v_p meters/sec. The wavelength is λ, and the relationship we saw earlier holds: $v_p = f\lambda$. v_p will be close to the velocity of light, but slightly less, depending on the type of the transmission line. There must also be a voltage wave flowing down the line with a peak value of V volts. We define the *impedance* of the line $Z=V/I$. Z may be a pure resistance, or it may be a resistance plus some capacitance or inductance.

Electric and Magnetic Fields

A more useful way of looking at the current and voltage waves is to consider the *fields* they produce. The charges and currents along the transmission line produce electric and magnetic fields as shown in Figure 2.34. Note that the electric (E) and magnetic (H) fields are always at right angles to each other, and both are at right angles to the direction of travel of the wave. This composite wave is called an electromagnetic (EM) wave. The fields carry the energy of the wave from the transmitter to the end of the line.

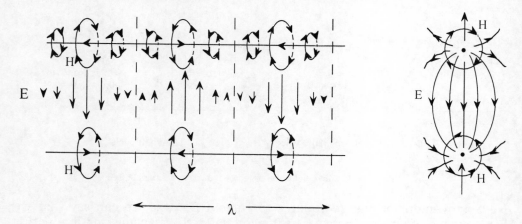

Figure 2.34. Current flow and E and H fields in a transmission line.

Characteristic Impedance

The ratio of the voltage to current at the input of a transmission line is called the *input impedance*, and the ratio at the output is called the *output impedance*. If the line were of infinite length, the *characteristic impedance*, Z_o, of the transmission line would be the ratio of the voltage to current on the infinite line. The characteristic impedance is purely resistive.

The characteristic impedance is important in determining how much energy will be transferred from the input to the output. If the line were infinitely long, all of the energy would be sent to the output and none would return. If the line is not infinitely long, it can be made to look as if it is by terminating it in a purely resistive load equal to the characteristic impedance. If the termination is any other load than Z_o, some of the energy will be reflected back to the input.

Voltage Standing Wave Ratio (VSWR)

If no antenna is connected, when the wave gets to the open circuit end, it sees a complete discontinuity - a sudden change to another medium - so it is reflected back towards the transmitter, which continues to send energy towards the open end. There are then two waves, travelling at the same speed in opposite directions. This produces a pattern that stands still, or a *standing wave*.

The incident and reflected waves will have peak values of V_{inc} and V_{ref} volts respectively. At some points these waves will add together and at other points will subtract from each other producing the peaks and troughs of the standing wave shown in Figure 2.35.

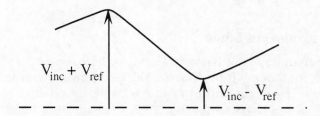

Figure 2.35. Creation of a standing wave.

The ratio of the peak to the trough is the Voltage Standing Wave Ratio (VSWR).

$$VSWR = \frac{V_{inc} + V_{ref}}{V_{inc} - V_{ref}}$$

If there was an open circuit (or a short circuit) at the far end, all the power would be reflected so that: $V_{inc}=V_{ref}$ and VSWR=∞. If there was a perfectly efficient antenna at the far end of the line, and all the power sent down the line was radiated into space, and there would be no reflected power. That is: $V_{ref}=0$ and VSWR=1.

If the VSWR=1, there is no standing wave, no reflected power and the antenna is said to be perfectly *matched* to the transmission line. If the VSWR=∞ there is a complete *mismatch* at the end of the line and no power is radiated at all.

VSWR can therefore have a value of between 1 and ∞, depending on how well matched the line is to the antenna. A VSWR of greater than 2 is always undesirable, since: all available power is not transmitted, which is inefficient; and power is flowing back into the transmitter, which can damage the set.

Desirable Features of Transmission Lines

Transmission lines are used widely to connect pieces of equipment and particularly to connect the transmitter and receivers to their respective antennas. Ideally, the transmission line should:

- have high capacity;
- have low attenuation;
- be matched to its termination to allow for maximum power transfer;
- have low crosstalk so that one transmission line is not affected by another;
- have low dispersion so that all frequencies travel at the same velocity;
- be able to cope with the required power levels;
- be easily handled and installed; and
- ensure personnel safety.

Types of Transmission Lines

There are two main types of transmission line: *balanced* and *unbalanced*. At any one time, balanced lines have voltages (and currents) on the two conductors that are equal and opposite relative to earth. Unbalanced lines have a positive or negative voltage on one conductor and the other conductor is earthed (at zero volts).

Balanced Transmission Lines

Two-Wire Line. Two-wire lines consist of two parallel conductors maintained a fixed distance apart. There are two main types.

- **Open two-wire line.** Figure 2.36(a) shows an open two-wire line. The balance is maintained by keeping the two wires apart by means of insulating bars, or spacers. The balance is easily disturbed, however, by nearby metallic objects and large radiation losses can be obtained.

- **Insulated two-wire line.** As illustrated in Figure 2.36(b), insulated two-wire line uses a solid dielectric between the conductors instead of air, and is therefore easier to install.

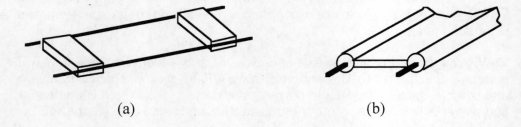

(a)   (b)

Figure 2.36. Two-wire (a) open line and (b) insulated line.

Twisted Pair. Twisted pair consists of two insulated copper wires twisted together to maintain the wires at a fixed distance apart. Twisting also limits radiation from the wires by aiding in the cancellation of the electric and magnetic fields and balances them against the effects of any induced radiation. Further reduction in both effects is often obtained by placing a screen around the twisted pair - called shielded twisted pair (STP). Twisted pair has relatively high losses, high radiation and low bandwidth, but is cheap and easy to install.

Multicore Cable. Multicore cable is made up of many twisted pairs that are shielded by a foil sheath. Each twisted pair is colour coded and the cable is often strengthened by non-conducting elements.

Unbalanced Transmission Lines

Coaxial Cable. As shown in Figure 2.37, a coaxial cable comprises two conductors that are separated by a dielectric, normally Teflon or polyethylene. The majority of electromagnetic field is restricted to the cable eliminating most radiation losses. The outer conductor also shields the inner wire from radiation from any RF sources in the vicinity. Coaxial cables can be used for frequencies up to 3GHz. They have lower attenuation and wider bandwidth than copper cables.

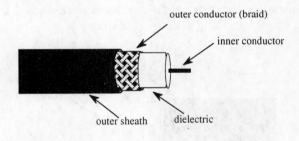

Figure 2.37. A coaxial cable.

Advantages and Disadvantages of Copper Transmission Lines

Advantages. Copper-based transmission media have always been used for communications systems. They are based on proven technologies and can be installed at low cost. They can carry high powers and are easy to use, join and terminate.

Disadvantages. However, copper cables have a number of significant disadvantages. They are heavy, particularly when deployed in large numbers; and suffer from significant crosstalk and large losses when used over more than short distances. They suffer from interference from RF sources along the path and transmission quality is reduced due to high-frequency limitations. These disadvantages are very important for transmission over medium to long distances requiring high bandwidth, and copper cable is now rarely used due to the high cost of providing a large number of cables and the large number of repeaters required. The preferred long-distance transmission medium is based on optical fibre technology.

Waveguides

So far, we have discussed media in which the signals travel as currents and voltages on two conductors. Waveguides, as their name suggests, provide a medium for signals to travel as electromagnetic waves inside a metal tube, which is normally rectangular. Waveguides of this form are usually only used at SHF and above. We will not consider them here, but we will briefly discuss a much more common waveguide - optical fibre.

Optical Fibre

An optical fibre is constructed by enclosing a thin glass fibre core (50-100μm) in a glass cladding (125-140μm) and surrounding the result in a protective jacket as shown in Figure 2.38. Electrical signals are translated into light pulses by modulating a laser and are detected at the receiver by photoelectric diodes. A waveguide for the optical frequencies is provided by the different refractive indices of the cladding and the glass core.

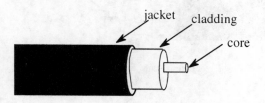

Figure 2.38. An optical fibre.

The propagation of the light along the core is analogous to the propagation of a current along a transmission line. The light will form standing waves and will propagate in a number of *modes*, which have different visible patterns. *Multi-mode fibres* allow a number of modes to propagate at the same time. The different modes mean that the signal arrives at the receiver at different times depending on the mode of propagation, which leads to degradation, called *signal dispersion*. A fibre that restricts propagation to a single mode is called *single-mode fibre*. Single mode is normally obtained by making the core small so that the rays strike the wall of the core at almost grazing angle.

Advantages. Optical fibres provide large bandwidth and can carry many times more signals than copper cables. Because there is such a low loss associated with the propagation of light in the fibre, optical fibres also provide extremely reliable long-distance communications. The fibres are light and small, making them ideal for installing in buildings and existing cable ducts. Since the information is contained in light energy, there is no RF radiation from optical fibres, nor are they affected by noise of interference in the areas through which there are run. The lack of radiation provides very secure communication whilst the immunity to noise and interference makes them ideal for use in heavy machinery workshops and similar locations. Since the signal in the fibre is not electrical, there are no earthing problems associated with installation.

Disadvantages. Although the raw material for optical fibres is plentiful and cheap, the propagation channel for the light is critical and is very hard to repair or join. The repair process requires that the core be precisely aligned and must ensure that the two cables abut perfectly and no dust or grime intrudes into the joint. Multiplexing is difficult with optical fibres so they are mainly used for high-capacity, point-to-point links. Similarly, the cables are very hard to terminate or to split to allow switching or tapping, compared with wire cables, which can be joined with a simple twist. However, if repair of a wire cable that had a similar capacity as optical fibre was to be considered, the repair of the fibre has a similar, if not better, repair time. The cost of fibre optic cable can be greater for short distances, but for distances greater than several hundred metres, fibre optic cables are cheaper for similar capacity since copper cable requires many more repeaters.

SUMMARY

This chapter has described the basic theory underlying communications systems. It has been necessarily brief, but has addressed the major issues necessary to understanding battlefield systems. The next chapter extends these concepts and addresses the fundamentals of radio propagation, which is the major means of communication on the battlefield.

3.
Propagation Fundamentals

RADIO-WAVE PROPAGATION

A radio wave is created when an alternating electric current is caused to flow in a rod or wire (the antenna). The alternating current produces an alternating magnetic field, which produces an alternating electric field and so on. This pattern of alternating fields moves out from the antenna as illustrated in Figure 3.1 for a sinusoidally varying current. The propagating wave is called a *transverse electromagnetic (TEM) wave* because the electric and magnetic fields are at right angles. The wave propagates in free-space at the speed of light.

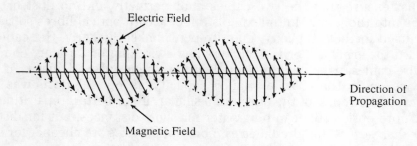

Figure 3.1. TEM wave.

Polarisation. The plane of the electric field is used to define the polarisation of the wave; if it is vertical the wave is said to be *vertically polarised* (as in Figure 3.1) and if it is horizontal, the wave is said to be *horizontally polarised*. Vertically polarised waves are launched from vertical antennas; horizontally polarised waves from horizontal antennas.

Radio communication techniques are normally categorised in accordance with the method of propagation used. Waves in close proximity to the Earth are called *ground waves*; those that rely on reflections from the atmosphere are called *sky waves*; and those that rely on scattered energy from atmospheric turbulence are called *scattered waves*. Frequencies from ELF to low HF propagate by surface wave, low to mid HF through sky wave, and high HF and above propagate through space wave.

Ground Waves. Figure 3.2 shows the RF energy transmitted as ground waves. Some of the energy will travel directly to the receiving antenna in *direct waves*. Some will be directed towards the ground, be reflected, and then received by the antenna. These are called *ground-reflected waves*. The combination of the direct and the ground-reflected waves is called *space wave*. Some energy will also be diffracted around ground features and is propagated by *surface wave*.

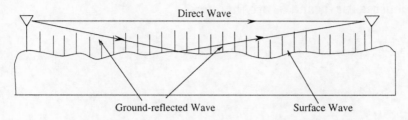

Figure 3.2. Ground-wave propagation.

Sky Waves. Space wave communications is generally limited to line-of-sight. The limit for surface waves is dictated by a number of considerations but is generally around 60-70km. Figure 3.3 shows that RF signals may be received beyond the horizon through the reflection of sky waves from the ionosphere.

Scattered Waves. Energy may also be received as scattered waves from turbulence in the troposphere. Scattered waves are also possible from turbulence in the ionosphere or from the ionised tails of meteors.

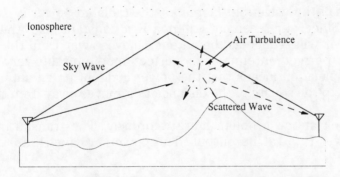

Figure 3.3. Sky-wave and scattered-wave propagation.

Space-Wave Communications

Let us assume that each antenna is an *isotropic radiator*; that is, a perfect antenna that radiates power equally in all directions. Let us also assume that the propagating medium is perfect, so there is no attenuation of the radiated power as it travels through space. Both of these assumptions are not strictly true and they will be modified later, but they serve as a good start point.

How much of that power will be incident at the receive antenna, a distance d away? Let's look at the spherically propagating wavefront shown in Figure 3.4.

At distance d_1 away from the antenna the wavefront consists of the transmitted power, P_t, spread over the surface area of a sphere ($4\pi d^2$). The power densities at d_1 and d_2 are therefore:

$$P_{den\,(d_1)} = \frac{P_t}{4\pi d_1^2} \quad \text{and} \quad P_{den\,(d_2)} = \frac{P_t}{4\pi d_2^2}$$

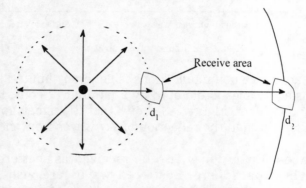

Figure 3.4. Spherically propagating wavefront.

As the radius of the wavefront increases, the radiated power is spread over a larger area. Since our receiving antenna is a constant size, the amount of incident power will reduce as the antenna moves away from the source. So, even with a perfect antenna in a perfect medium, the very process of spherical propagation means that the power incident on an antenna reduces in proportion to the square of the distance as it moves away from the source.

Let's now look at the problem more rigorously. The transmitter amplifier provides power P_{amp} at its output. The power provided into the antenna terminals is:

$$P_t = P_{amp} L_t$$

where L_t is the coupling loss between the transmitter and the antenna as a result of losses in the connectors and in the transmission line.

Radiating spherically is wasteful, since we normally want to increase the power radiated in a certain direction. We therefore need to modify our isotropic radiated power by taking into account the gain of the transmit antenna in the direction of the receiver. The result is called the *effective isotropic radiated power (EIRP)*:

$$EIRP = P_t G_t = P_{amp} L_t G_t$$

where G_t is the gain of the transmit antenna.

The EIRP is the power incident at the receiver as if an isotropic radiator had radiated it. In other words, we have identified the power (EIRP) that would have to be radiated from an isotropic antenna to achieve the same power incident at the receiver as that from our transmitter with an antenna gain of G_t.

Since we have assumed a perfect propagating medium, the power density of the propagated wave at a distance of d away is:

$$P_{den(r)} = \frac{EIRP}{4\pi d^2}$$

The propagating medium is not perfect so there will be a number of additional losses (L_a) due to a variety of reasons that we will discuss in greater detail later. Taking this into account:

$$P_{den(r)} = \frac{EIRP}{4\pi d^2} L_a$$

Rewriting in terms of the transmitter amplifier power gives:

$$P_{den(r)} = \frac{P_{amp} L_t G_t L_a}{4\pi d^2}$$

We have now calculated the *density* of power, in Watts per square metre (Wm^{-2}), arriving at the antenna. The power received, in Watts (W) is calculated by multiplying the power density by the antenna's effective receiving area A_e (called the *effective aperture*):

$$P_{ant} = P_{den} A_e \tag{3-1}$$

A_e is related to radiation wavelength and antenna gain:

$$A_e = \frac{\lambda^2}{4\pi} G_r$$

Again, the receive antenna is rarely an isotropic receiver but has a gain in the direction of the transmitter, G_r. Substituting for P_{den} and A_e, Equation (3-1) becomes:

$$P_{ant} = P_{amp} \underbrace{\frac{L_t G_t}{4\pi d^2} L_a}_{P_{den}} \underbrace{\frac{\lambda^2 G_r}{4\pi}}_{A_e}$$

which can be rewritten:

$$P_{ant} = P_{amp}\left(\frac{\lambda}{4\pi d}\right)^2 L_t G_t L_a G_r$$

since the factor $(\lambda/4\pi d)^2$ is known as the *free-space loss (FSL) factor*, discussed later.

This equation represents the power received by the receive antenna. This power still must be delivered to the receiver and will suffer attenuation due to coupling and mismatch losses (L_r) in the receive antenna cable. The total collected power at the receiver's terminals is therefore:

$$P_r = P_{amp}(FSL)L_t G_t L_a G_r L_r$$

(3-2)

Friis Formula. When both antennas are assumed to be lossless and no atmospheric losses are present, the equation is simplified to:

$$P_r = P_{amp}\left(\frac{\lambda}{4\pi d}\right)^2 G_t G_r$$

which is known as the *Friis formula*. This formula provides a quick assessment of the power received over a particular path. Of course, the actual power received will be less than this value but, since FSL is the largest loss, the Friis formula produces reasonable results for quick assessments. If the Friis formula predicts insufficient receive power then precise analysis is not necessary.

What we need to know is how much of the transmitted power will reach the receiver. This quantity is called the transmission path loss (TPL), the ratio of the received power to that generated by the transmitter's amplifier:

$$TPL = \frac{P_r}{P_{amp}} = (FSL)L_t G_t L_a G_r L_r$$

This equation can be rewritten, since the combination of free-space loss (FSL) and path propagation losses (L_a) is called the radio path loss (RPL) - the losses in the path (as opposed to the losses in the equipment at either end). That is:

$$TPL = (RPL)L_t G_t G_r L_r$$

The maximum transmission path loss (TPL_{max}) is a design measure nominated for a given system and represents the maximum loss that the system can accept before becoming unworkable. Since the antenna gains and losses are normally constant for a given system configuration, they can be grouped together as the system value S_v so that:

$$S_v = L_t G_t L_r G_r \quad \text{and} \quad TPL_{max} = (RPL_{max}) S_v$$

The viability of the radio path is ascertained, therefore, by calculating the RPL and determining if it is lower than RPL_{max}. This sounds simple but we have been very general so far in the treatment of path losses. Each of these will be dealt with in more detail in the following sections but, briefly, they are *free-space loss (FSL)*; *reflection loss (RL)*; *diffraction loss (DL)*; *clutter loss (CL)*; and *atmospheric loss (AL)*. For ease of calculation the RPL formula is written in the decibel format:

$$RPL = FSL + RL + DL + CL + AL \text{ (dB)} \qquad (3\text{-}3)$$

Equivalent Radius of the Earth

Before looking at the various loss factors, we need to examine the increase in range that arises because the atmosphere refracts the wave. In a uniform atmosphere, radio waves would travel in a straight line and the range would be limited by the horizon due to the curvature of the Earth.

However, the density of the Earth's atmosphere is not uniform and its refractive index decreases with height. Therefore, a radio wave travelling through the atmosphere will experience a gradual refraction, which will bend the wave slightly towards the ground as shown in exaggerated form in Figure 3.5(a). This curvature of the radio path increases the range of communications beyond the horizon. This is an advantage but makes it difficult to plot the radio path to determine a radio line-of-sight. To solve these difficulties a correction factor k is used, which effectively increases the radius of the Earth (r_a=6,379km) to become the *effective radius* r_e=kr_a. As shown in Figure 3.5(b), this compensates for the refraction and the radio path can be drawn as a straight line.

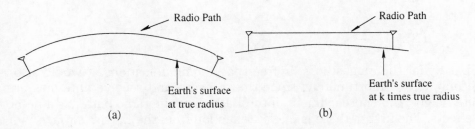

Figure 3.5 Correction of Earth radius by k factor.

The value of k depends on a number of factors and fluctuates, even under normal weather conditions. At VHF, a value of k=4/3 is used. At SHF, refraction is normally negligible so a value of k=1 is used. Figure 3.6 illustrates special corrected paper that is available to plot path profiles.

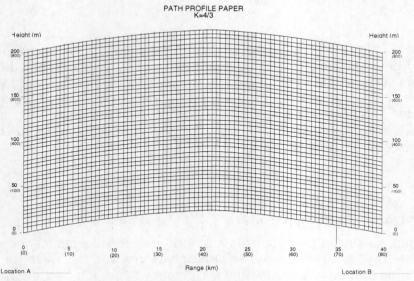

Figure 3.6. Path profile paper (k=4/3).

The *radio horizon* (for k=4/3) can then be determined as:

$$d_{radio} = 4.12\left(\sqrt{h_T} + \sqrt{h_R}\right)$$

where d_{radio} is in kilometres and h_T and h_R are in metres.

Free-space Loss

We saw earlier that only a fraction of the power of an isotropic antenna $(1/4\pi d^2)$ will be incident on a receiving antenna. Further, the antenna aperture will only collect $\lambda^2/4\pi$ (with unity gain) of the incident power density. The combination of these two factors is free-space loss:

$$FSL = \left(\frac{\lambda}{4\pi d}\right)^2$$

FSL is by far the biggest loss. In free-space communications, it would also be the only loss. Unfortunately, since the transmit and receive antennas are a finite height, the encroachment of the Earth into the radio path has a number of effects. The first of these is due to reflection from the Earth's surface.

Reflection Loss

Figure 3.7 illustrates that when antennas are not in free space, the received signal will contain two components: the *direct* and the *ground-reflected wave*.

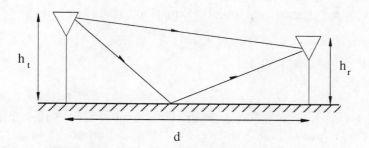

Figure 3.7. Direct and ground-reflected rays.

The reflected wave will suffer a phase change of:

$$\Delta = \frac{4\pi h_t h_r}{d\lambda}$$

so that the received power strength is:

$$P_r = P_{amp}G_tL_tL_aG_rL_r \underbrace{\left(\frac{\lambda}{4\pi d}\right)^2}_{\text{free-space loss}} \underbrace{\left|4\sin\left(\frac{\Delta}{2}\right)\right|^2}_{\text{reflection loss}}$$

This equation is similar to Equation (3-2) except for the additional reflection loss factor.

Plane Earth Loss Formula. At large distances Δ becomes small as d becomes large compared to antenna heights:

$$\Delta = \frac{4\pi h_t h_r}{d\lambda} \text{ is small for } d \gg h_t h_r$$

Since $\sin(x) \approx x$ for small arguments, Equation (10-42) becomes:

$$P_r = P_{amp} G_t L_t L_a G_r L_r \underbrace{\left(\frac{h_t h_r}{d^2}\right)^2}_{PEL}$$

(3-4)

Equation (3-4) is identical to Equation (3-3) except that FSL is replaced by the *plane-earth loss (PEL)* quantity. Note that Equation (3-4) approximates that the received power at a large distance is independent of wavelength. Note also that the plane-earth model implies the inverse fourth law with respect to distance.

Diffraction Loss

Diffraction occurs when an obstacle intrudes into the radio path as shown in Figure 3.8. The value of the received signal at R depends on its position on the line AB. When R is well down into the "shadow" region (at point A) the received signal effectively falls to zero. As R rises, the signal strength increases until at C the signal strength will be half the free-space value, since the observer at R will "see" half of the radiation.

As R rises above C into the illuminated region the received signal continues to increase as more of the radiation is "seen" by the receiving antenna. At a certain point, the signal strength will exceed the free-space value (E_0) and reach E'. Thereafter, the signal will oscillate in strength about the free-space value as the alternatively additive and subtractive interference zones are exposed. The oscillations gradually decrease as more zones are exposed and the signal strength will settle at the free-space value.

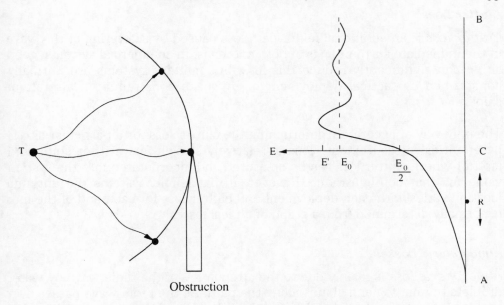

Figure 3.8. Effect of diffraction on received signal strength.

The reduction in the received signal strength below the free-space value, which occurs as a result of the obstruction is called *diffraction loss* and is calculated using a look-up table.

Egli's Formula. For propagation frequencies between 40MHz and 1GHz over irregular terrain (about 15m variation between hills and valleys) Egli approximated the received power to be:

$$P_R = \underbrace{P_{amp}G_tL_tL_aG_rL_r\left(\frac{h_th_r}{d^2}\right)^2}_{\text{PEL}} \underbrace{\left(\frac{40}{f}\right)^2}_{\substack{\text{Egli estimate}\\\text{of diffraction loss}}}$$

where range (d) and antenna heights are in metres, powers in Watts, and frequency in MHz.

Egli's formula is similar to the PEL formula from Equation (3-4) except for the last frequency-dependent term, which is empirically developed and accounts for diffraction loss over the stated type of terrain for the given frequency range. Care must therefore be taken to apply Egli's formula only within those constraints.

Clutter Loss

Clutter loss is an additional minor path loss caused by scattering of the wave in the immediate surroundings of both antennas. In commercial systems, good siting can significantly reduce this loss, but military systems are normally constrained by tactical deployment or by space constraints on aircraft or ships.

The only way of accurately determining the clutter loss for a particular site is by empirical measurement. This is relatively straightforward for ships and aircraft where clutter loss can be measured and incorporated into the system value for that configuration. However, in battlefield systems the antenna location varies with each deployment and clutter loss for each end of the link is normally determined from a graph of typical losses.

Atmospheric Losses

Atmospheric loss is mainly due to the attenuation of the radio wave by water droplets of rain, fog and clouds along the path. As the radio wave passes over each spherical droplet, the droplet absorbs part of its energy and part is scattered. The degree of attenuation is a function of frequency, drop diameter, the drop dielectric constant, and the number of drops per unit volume. The attenuation is only appreciable when the droplet diameter is similar to the propagation wavelength. Atmospheric loss is therefore only significant above 10GHz, where its value is roughly proportional to precipitation rate.

Radio Path Loss Assessment

Each of the individual path losses can then be combined to form the radio path loss (RPL) calculated from Equation (3-2). The maximum radio path loss that can be sustained (RPL_{max}) is known for a given system. So, if $RPL <$ RPL_{max}, the *shot is workable*, if $RPL \approx RPL_{max}$ the *shot is marginal*, or if $RPL > RPL_{max}$ the *shot is unworkable*.

Surface-Wave Communications

As shown in Figure 3.9, surface wave travels as a vertically polarised wave along the surface of the ground, with the ionosphere and the ground acting as two sides of a waveguide. The wave is supported by currents flowing in the ground and follows the surface of the terrain. Surface wave has a short range as it is attenuated very heavily depending on ground conductivity and wave polarisation.

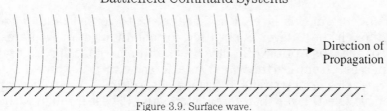

Direction of
Propagation

Figure 3.9. Surface wave.

The ground is not perfectly conducting, and some energy will be lost in the ground currents. Seawater has a high conductivity and provides good surface wave. Fresh water and wet soil provide fair conductivity. Dry, rocky terrain has poor conductivity. Other terrain such as urban environments and jungle provide poor conductivity due to the absorption of the wave by buildings and vegetation.

The absorption of energy in the ground slows the wave as it touches the ground, causing the wave front to tilt forward. Surfaces with poor conductivity cause high loss and greater tilt and finally total absorption. Angle of tilt also increases with increase in frequency. As the frequency increases, the utility of surface wave decreases so that surface-wave frequencies are normally limited to between 2MHz and 5MHz. Ranges are limited to approximately 30km for dry, rocky soil; 50km on good, moist farm soil and 150km across seawater.

In addition to ground type, terrain shape and vegetation cover must be considered. Small variations in terrain have little effect, as the surface wave will follow the shape of the ground. However, large variations will have a screening effect on propagation and will severely reduce range. Vegetation cover also attenuates surface wave, particularly when wet. Sparse bush-land will not provide significant additional attenuation but in jungle vegetation, surface wave is almost non-existent due to heavy absorption by foliage.

Sky-Wave Communications

Sky-wave communications cover large distances by utilising the ionosphere to refract waves back to Earth. The upper atmosphere consists mainly of nitrogen, oxygen and nitric oxide molecules, which undergo *ionisation* by ultra-violet radiation from the sun to produce positive ions and negative electrons. At night, in the absence of ultra-violet radiation, *recombination* of free electrons and ions reduces the level of ionisation. The ionisation process forms a number of layers since the gases in the upper atmosphere tend to lie in layers, each ionised by a different band of ultra-violet radiation.

D Layer. The D layer extends from approximately 50km to 100km. It is the least ionised region that exists during daylight hours only. Although some refraction occurs in this layer, it is insufficient to return radio waves to the Earth. Although the D layer is not used for communication, it is responsible for most of the absorption of a sky wave and also contains a great deal of noise generated from Earth, which interferes with the wanted signal. The lower frequencies are most affected since absorption is inversely proportional to frequency. The D layer therefore dictates the lowest frequency that can be used. The absence of the D layer at night is principally responsible for the better sky-wave communications that occur at night time.

E Layer. The E layer exists mainly during daylight and is weakly ionised at night. It has a higher density of ionisation than the D layer and extends from approximately 100km to 140km above the Earth. Sufficient refraction is provided to return the lower HF waves to Earth and the layer is used for most short-range HF communication during the day.

F Layers. Two well-defined F layers are present during daylight hours: the F1 layer (140km to 250km); and the F2 layer (250km to 400km). Both layers are more heavily ionised than the E layer and are capable of refracting all HF waves. The F layer is the principal medium for long-range and night time HF communications.

Radio waves travel in straight lines if the medium through which they pass has a constant density. As a wavefront enters the ionosphere it begins to follow a gradual curved path since the velocity of the wavefront is slightly reduced under the influence of the free electrons, thus causing a refraction of the wave. If there is a sufficient number of electrons, the path of the wavefront is bent back towards the Earth. If the frequency is gradually raised, a frequency will be found beyond which the waves will not be refracted sufficiently to return to Earth. These waves will continue up to the next layer, or, in the case of the F2 layer, on out into space.

Figure 3.10 illustrates that the refraction process is often considered to be a reflection process with the *actual height* of the refractive ionosphere replaced by a hypothetical *virtual height* of the reflective ionosphere.

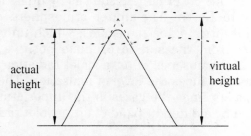

Figure 3.10. Actual and virtual ionosphere heights.

The range of sky-wave communications varies and is determined by three main factors: the *frequency* used, the *propagation angle*, and the *power* of the transmitter.

Frequency. If the frequency is raised, a higher layer will refract the wave. For example, refraction from the E layer will lead to a shorter range than from the F layer. The distance between the transmitting antenna and where the first useable sky wave returns to earth is called the *skip distance*.

Propagation Angle. The *propagation angle* (Δ) of a sky wave transmission is the angle between the wave and the ground. As illustrated in Figure 3.11, the lower the propagation angle the greater the communication range.

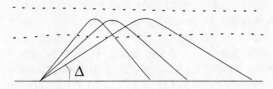

Figure 3.11. Range increase with decreasing propagation angle.

Power. Single-hop sky wave is limited to approximately 3,500km. If transmission power is increased, range is increased due to the occurrence of multiple hops of the transmission. As the wave is refracted back to Earth, it has sufficient power to be reflected back up to the ionosphere where it is again refracted. Worldwide communications are achieved in this manner. Although increasing power will increase range, it is not a very effective way of improving communications over a single-hop link. Better results can be obtained by changing frequency and using another layer.

Skip Zone. HF communication is possible in both the surface wave and sky wave modes. Because surface wave has limited range and there is a minimum value of skip distance for useable sky-wave communications, there often exists an area, called the *skip zone* or the *dead zone*, between the point where the surface wave diminishes and where the first useable sky wave returns to earth. HF communication is not possible to stations in this region. However, where there is a good conducting surface, such as over seawater, there may not be a skip zone and the receiving antenna may receive both ground and sky wave. In this case, judicious use of antennas is required to prevent the two signals from interfering.

The Best Frequency

As the frequency of a vertically incident wave is increased, the wave will penetrate higher before returning. The highest frequency that will return to

Earth from a vertical incidence transmission is called the *critical frequency*, f_o. As the ionosphere moves, the critical frequency will change and is therefore not useable for communications. A more reliable frequency must be found.

The *lowest useable frequency (LUF)* will be dictated by the level of absorption and noise in the D layer. The LUF is sometimes known as the *absorption-limiting frequency (ALF)*. Accurate prediction of the LUF is difficult due to variations in D-layer properties.

Since lower frequencies are attenuated more than high frequencies, it is desirable to choose the highest possible frequency. The highest possible frequency of operation at any angle is the *maximum useable frequency (MUF)*, which is normally dictated by the level of ionisation in each layer. The MUF is generally defined as the highest frequency that is available for use over a particular path for 50% of the time. However, a circuit that uses the MUF will experience heavy fading so, to produce a useable frequency, the MUF is reduced by a margin of 15% to provide the *optimum working frequency (OWF)*. The OWF is also called the *practical upper limit (PUL)* or the *optimum traffic frequency (OTF)* and is defined as the highest frequency available for use over the circuit for 90% of the time.

The key then is to calculate the critical frequency from which the MUF and the OWF can be obtained. Obviously, the mid-point of the path will be the portion of the ionosphere responsible for refraction of the wave. This mid-point is therefore called the *control point* for the link. Using the trigonometry of Figure 3.12, the MUF is related to the critical frequency:

$$MUF = \frac{f_o \sqrt{h^2 + x^2}}{h}$$

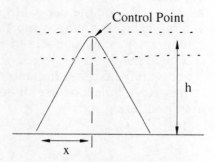

Figure 3.12. Sky-wave control point.

Calculation of MUF/OWF therefore requires calculation of the critical frequency and height of the control point for a particular path. Fortunately, critical frequency and control point heights are being measured and the appropriate frequencies are predicted continuously around the world and information charts like Figure 3.13 are produced.

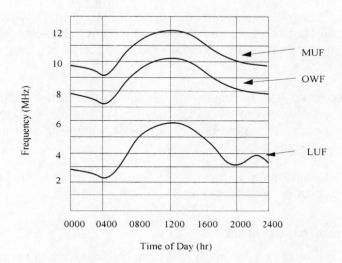

Figure 3.13. OWF chart.

Ionospheric Variations

The ionosphere suffers a number of variations that have a significant effect on sky-wave communications.

Geographical. There is obviously more ultra-violet radiation at the equator than at the poles. There is also an east-west variation. It is therefore important to ensure that predictions charts are for the correct area.

Seasonal. Winter and summer critical frequencies will vary due to variations in layer height. This is due to different quantities of ultra-violet radiation and the expansion and contraction of the atmosphere.

Daily. The critical frequency is higher during the day than at night. Daily variations are generally predictable and are accounted for in prediction charts.

Sunspot Cycle. Sunspots are dark patches on the surface of the sun that emit large quantities of ultra-violet radiation. So when there are more sunspots, ionisation densities are higher leading to higher critical frequencies and MUFs. Sunspots increase and decrease in fairly regular cycles - sunspot sunspots, ionisation densities are higher leading to higher critical frequencies and MUFs. Sunspots increase and decrease in fairly regular cycles - sunspot maxima occur every 11 years approximately. Frequency prediction charts take account of the sunspot cycle. A shorter, regular sunspot cycle occurs every 27 days as the sun rotates.

Solar Flares. These flares, more prevalent in high sunspot years, cause so much ionisation that the D Layer absorbs all frequencies. Sky wave can be blacked out for several hours by solar flares, which obviously only occur during the day.

Magnetic Storms. Storms create turbulence in the ionosphere and cause severe fading on all sky-wave links. Magnetic storms can last for days and occur during the day or night. Like solar flares, magnetic storms are more prevalent in years of high sunspot activity.

Sporadic 'E'. Occasionally clouds of dense ionisation occur in the E Layer and severely disrupt communications.

Advantages and Disadvantages

Advantages. Sky-wave communications have the following advantages:

- long-range communications are available with portable and mobile radios;
- both net communications and point-to-point links can be established;
- relatively low-cost antennas and terminal equipment are required;
- the transmission medium (the ionosphere) is difficult to interrupt; and
- sky-wave communications can be degraded gracefully in that the same communications system can be used for voice and data at reasonable speeds down to low-speed Morse Code.

Disadvantages. Sky-wave communications have the following disadvantages:

- limited available spectrum leads to a limited number of channels;
- channels are available worldwide with a large number of users possible;
- limited channel bandwidth leads to low data rates;
- channel use is time-variant and significant management is required; and
- the long wavelengths at sky-wave frequencies require large antennas.

Scattered-Wave Communications

Scattered-wave techniques make use of the turbulence in the troposphere or the ionosphere or ionised meteor tails. Ionospheric scatter and meteor burst techniques are not often used. Troposcatter techniques are, however, used in commercial and military communications networks.

Troposcatter

A troposcatter path can vary from about 100km to 1,000km. Most current systems, however, have ranges of between 150km and 400km. The maximum path attenuation is very high, so high transmitter powers; low-noise, sensitive receivers; and high-gain parabolic antennas are normally required.

Normal RF power outputs are 100W, 10kW and 1kW, commonly 1kW. Antennas are parabolic with diameters ranging from 2-3m for transportable systems to 30m or 40m for static systems. Low-noise receivers are normally employed.

The frequency band of operation is between about 300MHz and 5GHz. Early troposcatter systems provided analogue FM communications in the 345-988MHz band. Digital systems require more bandwidth and operate in either the 1.7-2.1GHz or the 4.4-5.0GHz bands.

Troposcatter systems use diversity techniques in which a number of radio receivers receive independent samples of the RF signal and combine them to obtain a more stable output signal. Diversity operation can incorporate frequency, space, time and polarisation diversity. Frequency diversity provides a transmission on several frequencies simultaneously and the receiver selects the strongest. Space diversity utilises a number of separate antennas; time diversity sends the same information over the same link at different times; and polarisation diversity sends the same information using both vertical and horizontal polarisation.

Analogue troposcatter systems have a traffic capacity of 6-120 telephone channels. Higher capacities are generally not recommended because the propagation mechanism generates non-linear noise in the channels, limiting the bandwidth. FM is always used. Digital FSK or PSK troposcatter systems can transmit a bit stream of up to 2-3Mbps.

Advantages. The main advantages of troposcatter systems are:

- They permit a long path, using a single hop (five or six times a line-of-sight link) that fits neatly between line-of-sight systems and satellite systems and provides much more bandwidth than HF systems.
- They can be used on difficult terrain such as in:
  - connection between remote sites such as those in the desert or jungle;
  - connection of a remote island or oil rig to the mainland;
  - connection across uncontrolled territory or over difficult terrain; and
  - sabotage at repeater stations that are difficult to protect and resupply.
- Coverage of large areas can be obtained with only a few repeaters.
- Fewer frequencies and less maintenance are required because of the smaller number of stations.

- Security is easier to achieve as there are fewer stations to protect.
- Through-life costs are reduced because of the lower number of repeaters with operators, associated buildings, access roads, power plants, spares, test equipment, maintenance personnel etc.
- Narrow beam antennas provide a high immunity to interception.

Disadvantages. The main disadvantages are:

- The initial procurement cost is high, although the troposcatter solution may be the most cost-effective choice as the overall costs (investment, operation and maintenance during the life of the link) may be less than any alternative.
- High-gain antennas are difficult to orientate.
- Antennas must have a clear view of the horizon.
- There is a high RF hazard from the antennas.
- Mobile operation is costly due to the need to protect the sensitive transmitters, receivers and antennas required.
- There is a risk of interference over a wide area if frequencies are re-used by other stations.

ANTENNA FUNDAMENTALS

An antenna is a device for radiating or receiving electromagnetic waves. It is used to connect the transmitter and receiver to the communications channel, through which the electromagnetic wave will propagate.

Resonant Antennas

Earlier we saw how electromagnetic radiation is passed along a transmission line. The line is connected to the radio set and the far end is modified to release the radio energy. The "modified" section of the line is an antenna, and the process of releasing the radio energy is called *radiation*. Although, radiation applies specifically to transmitters, the reverse process applies to receivers. Fortunately, in almost every case, the properties of an antenna when receiving are the same as when radiating or transmitting, and often the same antenna is used for both purposes.

Resonant antennas have a standing wave on them. The problem is how best to launch the wave into space.

The Dipole Antenna

Figure 3.14(a) shows a transmission line that carries equal and opposite currents every half cycle. Between the two sides, the fields will be equal and opposite, and will therefore cancel.

As shown in Figure 3.14(b), we can open the ends to create two radiating elements A and B since equal and opposite fields are not produced in these regions. Further, the current in A is in the same direction as B so that the radiation from each will be in phase and will add rather than cancel.

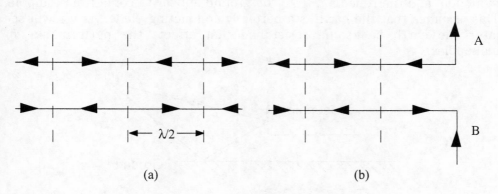

Figure 3.14. Currents in a transmission line.

As shown in Figure 3.15(a), if we fold back less or equal to half a wavelength in each leg, then the currents in each leg will still be in phase. Obviously we want to fold back as much as we can since the amount of radiation generated will be proportional to the current in the leg. But Figure 3.15(b) shows that if we fold back more than half a wavelength, the current in each leg is reduced since there are two out-of-phase currents cancelling out the fields.

This antenna, called the *dipole*, is the basis of many antennas. The best dipole is one with legs that are half wavelength long. The total length of the dipole is then one wavelength and is called a full-wave dipole.

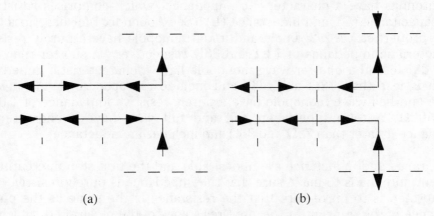

Figure 3.15. Transmission line with legs of (a) $<\lambda/2$ and (b) $>\lambda/2$.

The Monopole

A monopole is simply half a dipole. The other half is provided by induced currents in the ground, and is known as the 'image antenna' as shown in Figure 3.16. The image occurs since, at a distant point, the radiation from the monopole and the reflection from the ground appear to come from a dipole. This assumes that the earth is a perfectly conducting plane. As we will see later the earth has some resistance that affects the performance of monopoles.

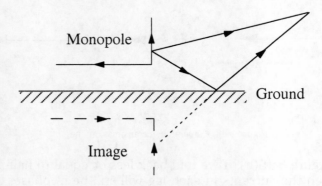

Figure 3.16. A monopole.

Antenna Properties

The following sections describe a number of properties of an antenna.

Input Impedance

All antennas have a characteristic impedance, which comprises resistance (R), capacitance (C), and inductance (L). (See Appendix I for descriptions of these properties.) A λ/2 dipole and a λ/4 monopole have a purely resistive characteristic impedance of 72Ω and 36Ω respectively. A shorter than half-wave dipole and a quarter-wave monopole have a characteristic impedance which is less than 72Ω and 36Ω and includes a capacitance. A full-wave dipole and half-wave monopole have a purely resistive impedance of 1,000Ω and 500Ω. Antennas between half and full-wave have a characteristic impedance greater than 72Ω and 36Ω and includes an inductance.

Capacitance and inductance are undesirable and the first step in creating an efficient antenna is to make sure that the impedance is purely resistive. The second step is to make sure that the resistance is the same as the output resistance of the transmitter (or input resistance of the receiver) to which the antenna is connected. If this is not so, a high VSWR will be set up causing poor antenna performance and possible damage to the set. If the antenna resistance is the same as the set resistance, the antenna is *matched* to the set.

Most military sets have an impedance of 72Ω so that they can be connected directly to a half-wave dipole. To connect a set to any other antenna, something must be put between the set and the antenna to convince the set that it is working to a pure resistance of 72Ω. This task is usually performed by an *antenna tuning unit (ATU)*. *Tuning* an antenna means getting rid of the capacitance or the inductance. This is done by putting capacitance or inductance in series with the antenna, of the correct value to get rid of the unwanted inductance or capacitance. The result is a pure resistance, although it will be somewhat less than the characteristic impedance of the antenna. *Matching* then ensures that the characteristic impedance of the transmission line is equal to that of the antenna to ensure maximum energy transfer.

Radiation Pattern

The radiation pattern of an antenna is usually described by a Polar Diagram, which can be measured as illustrated in Figure 3.17. The receiver moves through 360° marking the received signal strength on radial lines of a circular scale. The points are joined together to create a polar plot.

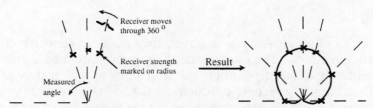

Figure 3.17. Antenna radiation pattern.

The polar diagram of a dipole in free space is shown in Figure 3.18. The maximum radiation is broadside on to the dipole with nothing coming out the ends. To get the three-dimensional picture, imagine the 'figure of eight' pattern rotating through 360°. The volume swept out by the figure would be a sort of doughnut, which if viewed end-on would appear circular. So, in that plane, the dipole is omnidirectional.

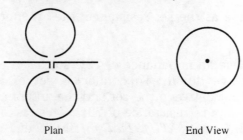

Plan   End View

Figure 3.18. Dipole radiation pattern.

Radiation patterns of antennas are significantly affected by the proximity of the ground or other objects. Generally, as the antenna is raised above the ground, more power is radiated upwards and communication can be achieved over greater distances.

Gain

An antenna has *gain* if it radiates more power in one particular direction than an isotropic radiator. Gain is usually measured relative to a dipole, and is measured in dB:

$$G = \frac{\text{power radiated by antenna}}{\text{power radiated by reference dipole}}$$

Bandwidth

The bandwidth of an antenna is the frequency range over which the antenna will perform effectively. The bandwidth of resonant antennas is small because they respond only to one frequency, the frequency at which they are $\lambda/2$ long - rather like an organ pipe only producing a note of one frequency. To change frequency using a dipole, the antenna must be pulled down and re-cut it to $\lambda/2$ at the new frequency. For a mast or whip, the ATU must be re-tuned. As we will see later, some antennas are broadband and are designed to have the same input impedance over a wide range of frequencies.

Antenna Efficiency

The radiation resistance R_R represents the power-radiating capacity of the antenna. The loss resistance R_L represents the actual conductor resistance of the antenna and the antenna leads. *Antenna efficiency* is the ratio of the power dissipated in the radiation resistance to that radiated in both the radiation and loss resistances. The loss resistance will be increased enormously by bad joints or connections in the antenna or antenna lead. Dirt or grease between whip sections is an example. If the radiation resistance is low, as is the case in a 3m whip at 3MHz where R_R may only be 5Ω, it becomes important to keep R_L small. A bad joint could make $R_L = 100\Omega$, giving an efficiency of 4.76%, which is not good!

Current Distribution

The current distribution on a resonant antenna can be sketched as illustrated in Figure 3.19.

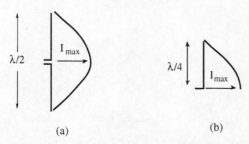

(a)   (b)

Figure 3.19. Current distribution (a) λ/2 dipole (b) λ/4 monopole.

Earth Resistance

A dipole can be replaced by a monopole over a perfectly conducting plane. The real earth is not perfectly conducting and always has some resistance, depending on the moisture and mineral content of the soil. Earth resistance will have the effect of reducing the amount of reflection in the ground so that the image appears to have less effect than the monopole and the antenna will not have the same radiation pattern as a dipole. The second effect of earth resistance is to increase the resistance of the antenna, thereby reducing its efficiency.

The resistance of the earth normally varies from 10Ω when the earth wire is soldered to a main water pipe near the ground to about 100Ω obtained from a moderate earth connection. The radiated power is reduced by one third if the earth resistance increases from 10 to 100Ω.

Better results can be obtained if an 'artificial' perfectly conducting earth is provided. This *counterpoise* or *earth mat* is normally constructed from a set of radial copper wires; at least four wires are required, each not less than 4m long. It is better to have more short wires than fewer long ones. A counterpoise should always be used, unless prevented by the tactical situation.

Travelling Wave Antennas

Resonant antennas have a current standing wave on them, even if there is none on the feeder. Figure 3.20(a) shows that an end-fed half wavelength antenna has the same polar diagram as a half-wave monopole. Figure 3.20(b) illustrates the polar diagram if the length of the end-fed antenna is increased to a full wavelength.

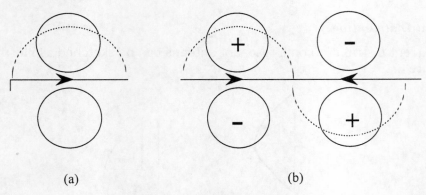

(a)   (b)

Figure 3.20. Polar diagram for end-fed antennas.

Each half-wavelength section has a similar polar diagram, but because of the reversal of current, the one on the right is out of phase with the one on the left, producing zero power at right angles to the antenna, as illustrated in Figure 3.21(a). Carrying this principle further, Figure 3.21(b) shows the polar diagram for a wire 6λ long. As the wire is increased in length, the main lobes get bigger and closer to the wire, and the minor lobes multiply.

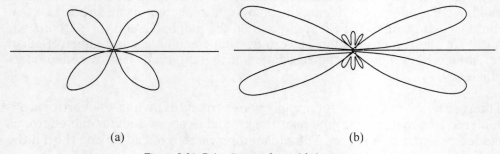

(a)   (b)

Figure 3.21. Polar diagram for end-fed antennas.

If the wire is terminated in a resistance equal to the characteristic impedance of the wire, the lobes A and B shown in Figure 3.21 cancel out. Now the antenna is directional, the three-dimensional polar diagram of which looks like a vase coaxial with the wire.

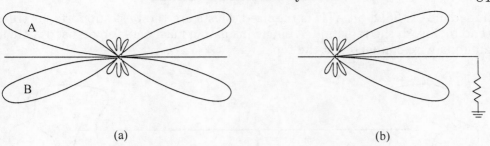

(a)   (b)

Figure 3.22. Polar diagram (a) before and (b) after termination.

A single end-fed wire is not often used as an antenna. End-fed wires are more usually arranged as an *inverted V, sloping V,* or *rhombic antenna* as discussed in the following sections.

HF Surface Wave Antennas

The Dipole

The dipole is the ideal omnidirectional antenna for field use. It has an input impedance of 72Ω and therefore doesn't need an ATU. However, surface waves are vertically polarised and use a relatively low frequency. These two criteria provide a few problems. The height of an efficient vertical half-wave dipole, as illustrated in Figure 3.23, would have to be 50m at 3MHz. Unfortunately, in the field, it is rare to find trees that high. However, the half-wave dipole is useful if it can be erected, as it can be at least twice as efficient as the quarter-wave monopole, which is discussed next.

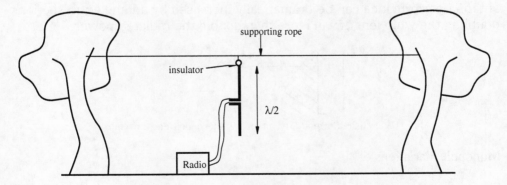

Figure 3.23. A half-wave dipole.

The Monopole

The next best antenna, the quarter-wave monopole (or Marconi antenna), can still be 25m high for 3MHz. Additionally, because a monopole's input impedance is 36Ω, an ATU is required. Masts are the best supports, as trees tend to absorb the radiation. A single insulating mast can also be used with an antenna wire connected at the top.

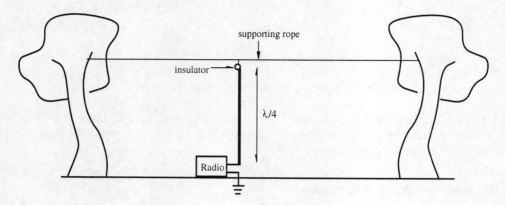

Figure 3.24. Quarter-wave vertical antenna.

HF Surface Wave Whips

For many mobile applications, a 25m monopole is still too large. In these cases a vertical rod antenna is used. However, any reduction in the length of the monopole will reduce the radiated power. Therefore, for antennas shorter than a quarter-wave, more transmitter power is required to achieve the same radiated power. Figure 3.25 illustrates the extreme case for a 3m whip where the current on the antenna is only the tip of the distribution and most of the power is absorbed in the ATU. When the vehicle stops for any length of time, antenna performance can be dramatically increased by adding extra sections - doubling the whip length will more than double the radiated power.

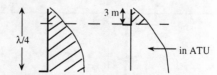

Figure 3.25. Current distribution in λ/4 monopole and 3m whip.

Monopole Variations

Shortening the quarter wave monopole wastes most of the power in the ATU. A number of HF surface wave antennas have been developed to reverse this wastage and to get λ/4 worth of current distribution to produce surface wave with less than λ/4 height. Figure 3.26 illustrates the (a) *sloping wire*, (b) *inverted 'L'*, and the (c) *'T' antennas*.

The *sloping wire antenna* is more efficient than a vertical wire of the same height and is easier to erect. However, radiation is no longer omnidirectional and sky wave is radiated as well as surface wave, unnecessarily increasing the opportunity for intercept. The upper end of the antenna should be as high as possible to reduce sky wave. The *inverted 'L' antenna* is an omnidirectional antenna that is more practical than a vertical wire at lower frequencies and is more efficient than a rod or wire at the same height. The vertical portion should be as long as possible as the horizontal portion will radiate sky wave. The *'T' antenna* is similar to the inverted 'L' except that the top portion is bent over into two arms of equal length. For its height, this is the best surface wave antenna that has the added advantage that it does not radiate any sky wave since the currents in the horizontal arms cancel out.

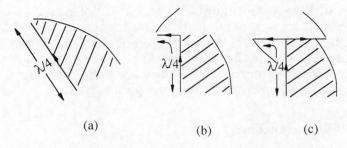

(a)   (b)   (c)

Figure 3.26. Monopole variations.

HF Sky-wave Antennas

Most HF sky-wave antennas are variations of the horizontal dipole placed at appropriate heights above the ground to produce varying take-off angles. However, some monopoles are also used for sky wave.

For short ranges (0-300km) the take-off radiation angle must be between 60° and 90°. This can be achieved with a horizontal, half-wave dipole; a quarter-wave; or a three-quarter wave travelling wave antenna.

For medium ranges (300-1,500km), radiation angles are required between 60° and 20°. Depending on the exact angle required, there are several possibilities. Horizontal half-wave dipoles between 0.25λ and 0.6λ above the ground can give angles of radiation between 60° and 25° - these are bi-directional, however, which can be wasteful. The vertical monopole can also be useful for these ranges, although it is omnidirectional, which may be undesirable in a hostile environment. Where time and space permit, the most useful antenna for medium ranges is the sloping 'V' antenna, which consists of two wires, several wavelengths long, arranged in a horizontal V with the apex elevated. The legs of the V are terminated in 300Ω resistors to eliminate standing waves, and the antenna is fed at its apex.

The sloping 'V' can have a range of up to about 2,000km. For greater ranges, radiation angles of 10° or less are required. There are various complicated arrays available, such as the rhombic antenna. All are very large, static and time-consuming to erect.

Alignment of Sky-wave Antennas. For short ranges the alignment of sky-wave antennas is not critical, except that in the tropics where antennas should be aligned north-south irrespective of the direction of working. Dipoles higher than a quarter wave above the ground should be broadside on to the direction of working. For distances greater than 1,000km, a great circle bearing must be used to align directional antennas.

Polarisation of Sky-wave Signals. Whatever its polarisation when it enters the ionosphere, a wave emerging from the ionosphere will have random polarisation, but probably showing a preference for the polarisation of the transmitting antenna. It is therefore possible to work vertically polarised to horizontally polarised antennas over a sky-wave link. In the field, the type of antenna chosen will normally determine the polarisation.

VHF Ground Wave Antennas

VHF antennas can be either surface wave or space wave antennas depending on how high they are above the ground. Whip antennas are mostly monopoles and are mainly used for surface wave.

Vertical Rod (Whip) Antenna. Rods and whips are robust and self-supporting and quick to erect. The set case or the vehicle chassis is used as the lower part of the antenna system. Radiation is omnidirectional. However, when mounted on a vehicle the direction of maximum radiation is diagonally across the bulk of the vehicle.

The Centre-fed Whip. The centre-fed whip illustrated in Figure 3.27 looks a monopole, but is in fact a dipole.

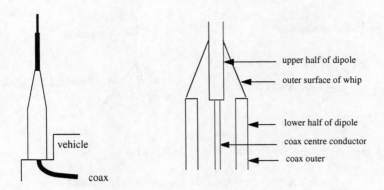

Figure 3.27. Centre-fed whip.

Vertical Half-wave Dipole. The half-wave vertical dipole is easily erected and dismantled and cheap to construct. It radiates mainly space wave and is omnidirectional.

Elevated Antennas

When an antenna is elevated, the reflection of the monopole in the earth does not occur to the same extent. It is therefore necessary to elevate an artificial ground plane with the antenna. However, the conductor provided as the ground plane has limited area. A greater proportion of high angle radiation is emitted as shown in Figure 3.28 where the radiation pattern is compared with that from a quarter-wave antenna on the ground.

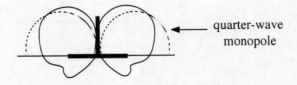

Figure 3.28. An elevated monopole antenna.

To overcome this, the flat conductor can be shaped like a cone as illustrated in Figure 3.29. This gives maximum radiation in the horizontal direction. In the field, it is not practicable to use a conical ground plane but reduced efficiency can be obtained using three wires spaced at 120° as shown in Figure 3.29(b).

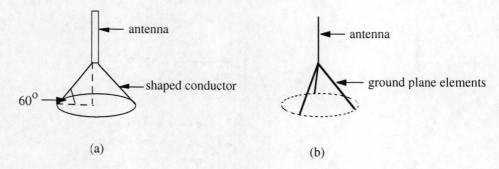

Figure 3.29. Elevated (a) conical and (b) wire ground plane.

Discone. By substituting a circular disc for the antenna section, the discone antenna becomes broadband. A cone is connected directly to the outer braid of the coaxial feeder and a disc is connected to the centre conductor as illustrated in Figure 3.30. The disc and the cone do not have to be of solid construction and may be constructed in cage form with separate wires to reduce weight.

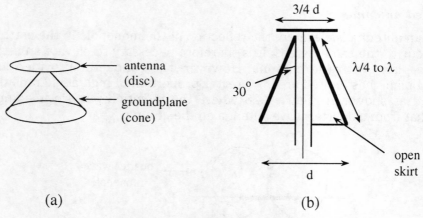

Figure 3.30. Discone antenna.

Array Antennas

Yagi Array. The Yagi antenna consists of a driven element (a dipole, or more commonly, a folded dipole), a reflector and a director. As illustrated in Figure 3.31, the director and reflector are both clamped to the support rod, as is the centre portion of the folded dipole. The Yagi produces a fairly narrow beam and is useful for directional links.

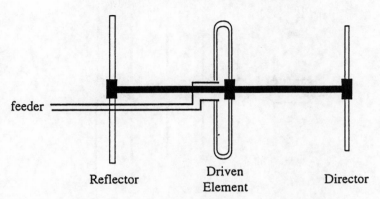

Figure 3.31. Yagi array.

Corner Reflector. The corner reflector antenna is predominantly used on line-of-sight radio relay links. It consists of a half-wave dipole in front of a corner reflector as illustrated in Figure 3.32(a). As shown in Figure 3.32(b), the reflector acts as a mirror and the resultant radiation pattern is the sum of the radiation patterns of the dipole and its images. The antenna has a similar radiation pattern to the Yagi with an average gain of about 9dB over a dipole.

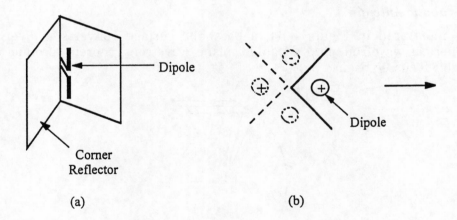

Figure 3.32. Corner reflector (a) construction and (b) images.

The Log Periodic. Figure 3.33 illustrates a log periodic antenna, which is designed so that, at the lowest frequency of operation, element f is resonant, and elements a to e act as directors. In the middle of the frequency band, element c will be resonant. Elements a and b will act as directors, d, e and f as reflectors. At the highest frequency, element a will resonate and the rest will act as reflectors. An end-fire radiation pattern is produced in the apex direction and is linearly polarised in the plane of the dipoles.

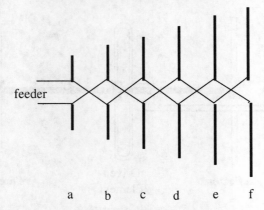

feeder

a   b   c   d   e   f

Figure 3.33. Log periodic antenna.

UHF / SHF Antennas

Propagation at UHF and SHF is characterised by line of sight paths, so beams must be very narrow, focussing as much energy as possible towards the target antenna. The most common antenna in these bands is the parabolic antenna.

Parabolic Antenna

As illustrated in Figure 3.34, a parabolic surface converts a diverging spherical wavefront into a parallel plane wavefront, thereby producing a highly focussed beam.

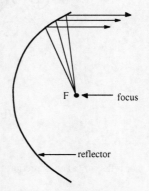

F ●◄——— focus

——— reflector

Figure 3.34. Parabolic reflector.

The gain (G) of a parabolic antenna of diameter D is:

$$G = (2\pi D / \lambda)^2$$

so that the larger the dish, the higher the gain.

SUMMARY

The last two chapters have covered the basic theory behind the components of the communication system introduced in Chapter 2. Communications have been assumed to be between any major type of source or sink using any analogue or digital means. One of the major requirements on the modern battlefield is the need to communicate between the information systems that support commanders. The fundamentals of these systems are the subject of the next chapter.

4.
Information Systems Fundamentals

INTRODUCTION

Traditionally, an organisation has managed three resources: capital, materiel, and labour (people). It is now widely acknowledged that a fourth resource, *information*, must also be managed to achieve effectiveness and efficiency.

Although most organisations have recognised the need for the management of information, many have confused *information management* with the provision of *information systems*. Many organisations have done little more than automate existing business practices. Whilst this has superficially resulted in reduced costs, results have been disappointing, as new technology has been applied to old methods without producing major benefits.

The first rule of automation is that current business practices should be examined critically since automated information systems make possible new business methods that would otherwise be impracticable. Adequate information management therefore starts with an understanding of business policies, methods of operation and performance measures. From this understanding, process and data models can be developed as a framework for information transfer and storage. Only then can appropriate information systems (hardware and software) be defined. However, more of this later. Let us first look at this thing called information and attempt to define it.

Information

An information processing system uses symbols to represent real world objects or ideas. The physical realisation of a piece of information in an information processing system might therefore be defined as *a pattern of symbols that has some real world meaning*. This definition implies that there is a rule we apply to the pattern to infer meaning. In fact, as we will see shortly, we use a number of different rules to infer meaning from the binary patterns stored by computer.

Data and Information. *Data* is the plural of the Latin word *datum*, which means 'fact'. Data then are facts, which are the raw material of information. Another definition of information then could be *data that has been ordered (again to convey some meaning)*. An example might be the results of a survey, which collects data about name, age, occupation, salary etc. This data is then converted into information, such as 'The average income for a storeman in the organisation is ....'.

The information held in an information system can generally be regarded as either *structured* or *unstructured*:

- **Structured information** is highly formatted and is held in databases, tables or spreadsheets. It is normally simple to define and is easily manipulated and analysed.

- **Unstructured information** is typically in the form of letters, memos, papers, minutes, plans, briefs, diaries, books, articles, audio tapes, images, videos etc. While unstructured information is often well formatted and well presented, the content does not lend itself to simple definition or easy manipulation and analysis. Access to unstructured information is therefore much more difficult in most organisations.

Generally, the higher in an organisation the less structured the information. Most organisations have information systems that can handle structured information but are much less able to handle unstructured information. This provides one of the considerable challenges to information management.

Information Management

Information management can be defined as:

The establishment and maintenance of processes, procedures and mechanisms (either manual or automated) necessary to ensure the accuracy, timeliness, accessibility, security and completeness of information.

As alluded to earlier, information management is too often confused with the process of information systems management, which depends on the particular hardware and software employed. Information management is a business process and is independent of hardware and software. Traditionally, the confusion has led to the automation of business processes through the purchase of hardware and software and an enforced translation of current business practices onto the new information system. This has often led to information systems driving business structures and methods - hardly an appropriate process. The reverse process is desirable; business methods and structures should dictate the types of information systems required. It is important to note here that the definition refers to processes, procedures and mechanisms that are *manual or automated*. Information management does not necessarily imply automation; manual procedures can sometimes provide the most efficient solution.

INFORMATION PROCESSING CONCEPTS

We saw in the previous chapter that we can choose patterns to have any meanings we wish. In an information processing system, we need to be able to represent the real world in symbols that can be stored and manipulated by a computer. In this section we will see that by using the simplest of devices, the two-state switch, we can represent and manipulate *numbers*, *characters* and *instructions* in a processing machine. We will then look at some models for information systems.

Two-state Devices

In early computers, a simple two-state switch was used to enter data. Modern computers use a transistor as a two-state switch, which is either on or off depending on the voltage level applied to it. Data is stored by using arrays of millions of transistors to provide storage for large quantities of data, often on one chip.

Such a data store is called a *memory* and patterns are represented by assigning the symbol "1" to a switch that is switched on and the symbol "0" to a switch that is switched off. The result is a series of 1s and 0s that represents a series of binary numbers.

For convenience, we group the binary numbers into different sized combinations as shown in Figure 4.1. A single element is called a *binary digit* or *bit* for short; four consecutive elements are called a *nibble* and eight consecutive elements are called a *byte*. Traditionally, a byte can be any length, but the most common practice is to use 8-bit bytes. Another unit is the *word*, which, in modern computers, is either 16 or 32 bits (that is, 2 or 4 bytes), although 32-bit word length is becoming much more common.

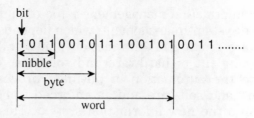

Figure 4.1. Bit, nibble, byte and word.

The word or byte groupings are also used to identify which particular location in the memory is being referred to. Each word or byte is associated with a unique address, which is a number ranging from zero to the maximum size of the memory. Each location in memory is accessed by its unique address to allow data to be written to and read from that location.

Modern computers have many thousands or millions of bytes in their memories, and memory size is referred to in terms of kilobytes (kbyte) or megabytes (Mbyte), where a kilobyte is 1,024 bytes and a megabyte is 1,048,576 bytes. These figures are the numbers that are the powers of two closest to one thousand and one million respectively.

Interpretation of Binary Patterns

We saw earlier that the computer can interpret the stored binary patterns either as numbers, characters or as instructions. The first two assist us to enter real world elements that we would like to manipulate. The third are the rules used by the computer to do the manipulation.

As illustrated in the simple information system shown in Figure 4.2, the heart of the system is the processor that manipulates patterns. An input device (probably a keyboard) sends data to the processor; an output device (probably a monitor screen) displays the processed information; a processing manipulates patterns, and some memory contains the processing rules and stores the data.

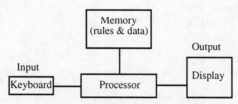

Figure 4.2. Information system model.

The processor interprets binary patterns held in memory as instructions or rules that give meaning to other patterns held elsewhere in the memory. Such a sequence of rules is called a *program* and the patterns representing the objects (numbers and characters) to be manipulated are called *data*.

Numbers

Patterns of 1s and 0s can naturally be associated with binary numbers, and this suited the first mathematical uses of computers. Although an information processing system is now used to do much more, mathematical calculations are still an important function in modern machines.

However, whilst the computer stores numbers in binary form, humans want the input and output to be in decimal form. That is not difficult to arrange since there is a direct relationship between the two numbering systems. With numbers one byte long, we can represent decimal numbers in the range 0 to 255. Using two bytes, the range becomes 0 to 65,535 and so on. Every extra bit added to the binary representation doubles the possible range of decimal numbers. The hardware within the computer contains the rules to manipulate binary numbers to perform arithmetic. The result is converted to a decimal number and displayed to the user.

Characters

The second type of patterns we want to store in the computer are characters. A standard mapping, called the American Standard Code for Information Interchange (ASCII), defines the patterns for 128 different characters, which are the letters and digits we require for the English language as well as a number of page layout characters. The 128 ASCII characters are defined by the seven-bit code shown in Figure 4.3.

MSB LSB	000	001	010	011	100	101	110	111
0000	NUL	DLE	SP	0	@	P	`	p
0001	SOH	DC1	!	1	A	Q	a	q
0010	STX	DC2	"	2	B	R	b	r
0011	ETX	DC3	#	3	C	S	c	s
0100	EOT	DC4	$	4	D	T	d	t
0101	ENQ	NAK	%	5	E	U	e	u
0110	ACK	SYN	&	6	F	V	f	v
0111	BEL	ETB	'	7	G	W	g	w
1000	BS	CAN	(	8	H	X	h	x
1001	HT	EM	)	9	I	Y	i	y
1010	LF	SUB	*	:	J	Z	j	z
1011	VT	ESC	+	;	K	[	k	{
1100	FF	FS	,	<	L	\	l	:
1101	CR	GS	-	=	M	]	m	}
1110	SO	RS	.	>	N	^	n	~
1111	SI	VS	/	?	O	˅	o	DEL

Figure 4.3. ASCII seven-bit code.

The most-significant bits (MSB) of the seven bits (that is the first ones) are listed across the top of the table and the least-significant bits (LSB) are listed down the side. The seven-bit code for the letter 'A', for example, is 1000001. Since characters are stored in an 8-bit byte, a '0' is added as the most significant bit, so 'A' is stored as 01000001. This spare bit can be used for error detection using a parity bit, as we discussed earlier.

Now if we can store a representation of any character in a single byte then we can store representations of any text or documents in a sequence of bytes. For example, text beginning with the words 'This is' is stored by placing the ASCII representations for the characters in seven adjacent bytes in the memory; shown in Figure 4.4 as bytes 15 through to 21. Then, by moving bytes and groups of bytes around in memory, we can move characters and text around in a document to perform word processing.

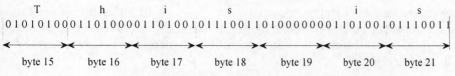

Figure 4.4. Binary representation of text characters.

Instructions

The last type of pattern is perhaps the most important: the instructions that represent the rules of interpretation and manipulation that give specific meanings to the data. A portion of memory in the processor is allocated to a *register* called the *program counter,* which holds the memory address of the next instruction. The program starts at a specified location and steps through the instructions, one at a time. These simple steps, performed at millions of instructions per second, allow large complex programs to be executed.

The Processor

The processor is usually called the *central processor unit (CPU)*. As illustrated in Figure 4.5, it consists of two main elements: the *control unit* and the *arithmetic and logic unit (ALU)*.

Control Unit

As its name implies, the control unit includes the computer's control program. It operates on the instructions in memory to initiate and control computer operations. The control unit is located in *Read Only Memory (ROM)*, which is a permanent memory on a chip that is encoded at the time of manufacture. The computer can read from ROM, but cannot alter it.

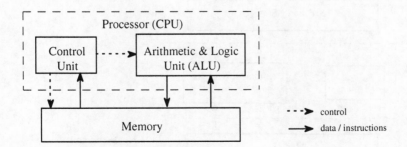

Figure 4.5. CPU components and memory.

Arithmetic and Logic Unit (ALU)

The ALU performs arithmetic and logic upon the data in accordance with the program instructions. The ALU can do three simple things: it can add and subtract numbers in binary; compare two pieces of data and decide on relative magnitude; and move data from one part of the computer to another. These simple operations are then combined to produce a large variety of others at great speed.

Memory

Memory is also known as *primary storage*, or sometimes as *main memory*. Memory holds instructions and data for processing by the CPU and it temporarily stores processed data before sending it to output devices. Like the CPU, memory consists of transistor circuits and is normally *Random Access Memory (RAM)*.

Random access means that the data can be accessed from memory in any order by simply quoting an address or addresses. This contrasts with the *sequential access* we will discuss in later sections, which is the way in which magnetic tape and some other storage devices have to be accessed by reading the data in a sequence, starting at the beginning.

Secondary Storage

Those instructions and data required immediately are always included in memory. However, not all data and applications can be stored in primary storage, as there is not sufficient room and access times would be too slow. Therefore, the information system needs some *secondary storage*, originally called a *backing store*. This storage is more permanent and has a greater capacity than primary storage. It is normally in the form of hard disk or CD-ROM. Figure 4.6 illustrates how the CPU accesses both primary and secondary storage.

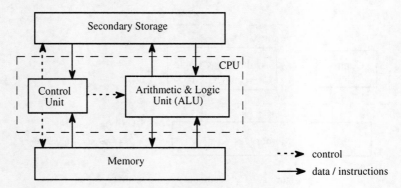

Figure 4.6. CPU access to primary and secondary storage.

Bus Types

Data and address transfer between the component parts of an information system occur across a *bus*. A bus comprises a number of digital lines, each of which moves one bit of data at a time. An 8-bit wide bus therefore has eight lines and can transfer one byte at a time. There are three types of bus: *address bus*, *data bus* and *control bus*.

Address Bus. An address bus carries addresses between the CPU and memory. The size of the address bus depends on the number of memory locations to be addressed. A common width for modern computers is 32 bits, which provides up to 2^{32}, or more than 4 billion locations. However, there is a continual drive to hold more data and larger programs in memory. Some computers are therefore beginning to appear with a 64-bit address bus.

Data Bus. The data bus transports data between memory and the CPU. The width of the data bus is proportional to the amount of data that has to be moved. Most modern computers, especially PCs, have 32-bit data busses. However, larger computers are beginning to appear with 64 and 128-bit data busses.

Control Bus. The control bus looks after control messages sent around the information system, doing housekeeping functions, controlling such activities as reads and writes to memory, input/output functions etc.

STORAGE

There are two main types of storage: magnetic storage (tape and disks), and optical discs.

Magnetic Storage Devices

Magnetic storage devices are based on the same storage principle as audio cassettes. A reading/recording head writes and reads magnetic field intensity on a magnetic medium, normally a metallic oxide attached to some substrate. Data is written by changing the magnetic field at the desired location and is read by observing the state of the field at that location.

Tapes

A magnetic tape is spooled through the heads so that data is written sequentially from one end to the other. Access is therefore sequential and can take some time, depending on where the data has been written. Although tapes can hold large amounts of data, their slow access speeds make them more suited to archival than to on-line access. This is particularly true since hard disk capacities are increasing rapidly.

Disks

Magnetic disks are the primary mass storage medium, although optical disks are beginning to take over. The disk stores information on circular tracks marked out on its surface. A magnetized spot on a track represents a '1' and a demagnetized spot a '0'. The disk rotates under an arm that moves a read/write head to the required track where it reads and writes data.

Access is not sequential like the magnetic tape. The appropriate location on the disk surface is specified and the head moves to that location and begins to read. This *random access* means that access to magnetic disks is much faster than tapes. There are two types of magnetic disk: *floppy disks* and *hard disks*.

Floppy Disks. Floppy disks are a cheap removable form of storage where a thin magnetic medium is encased in a protective plastic casing. Standard modern disks are 3.5-inch, high-density disks able to store 1.44 Mbytes of data. Higher capacities are becoming available and will no doubt become standard in the near future. Modern floppy drive formats can already store hundreds of Mbytes on a disk that is only slightly larger than a 3.5-inch floppy.

Hard Disks. Unlike floppy disks, hard disks are rigidly constructed and are heavier. To ensure reasonable access times, hard disks are constantly spun since they take several seconds to get up to speed. Hard disks are spun very quickly and the read/write heads are very close to the surface. Disks and heads are enclosed in an airtight casing to prevent dust particles from intruding between head and disk. Large capacities, up to 10 Gbytes, are available for internal mounting in personal computers. Multiple disks are spun and are read by multiple heads. Hard drives have much faster access speeds (up to two orders of magnitude greater) than floppy drives.

Optical Disks

Optical disks, or compact disks (CDs), operate on a similar principle to magnetic disks, except that a laser is used to read and write data on tracks on a light-sensitive medium. The laser writes data by burning small pits, which can then be read by laser. A pit represents a binary '1', and the absence of a pit a '0'. Light can be focussed very precisely so that tracks can be much closer than on a magnetic disk. CDs therefore have much greater capacity than magnetic disks, currently of the order of 600Mbytes. CDs provide a much more permanent storage than magnetic disks because CDs are not corrupted by magnetic fields and the size and the location of the pit does not vary with time. However, they do not have access times that are as fast as hard disks.

INPUT AND OUTPUT DEVICES

Input and output devices and secondary storage devices are generically called *peripherals*.

Input Devices

Input devices convert real-world information (text, data, voice and video) into the binary information that is processed within the computer.

Keyboard. The keyboard is still the primary device for entering information. The operator presses a key corresponding to the required letter or number and the appropriate binary characters are sent to the computer.

Mouse. The mouse, in its various forms, is now available with almost all computers. Movement of the mouse over the desktop controls the location of the pointer (or cursor) on the monitor screen. Whilst most software can still be used without it, a mouse is normally considered an essential tool for efficient software use.

Scanner. Scanners convert an image or a page of text into an image file within the computer. Images can then be stored and included with documents or presentations. Text images are further processed using optical character recognition (OCR) software to produce a text file.

Microphone. A microphone converts the spoken word or sounds into a digitized signal that can then be stored within the computer. This signal can be replayed when desired. The signal can also be converted to text through voice recognition software, although the state-of-the-art is not perfect. When voice recognition software can cope with the wide variation in speech patterns, the microphone will no doubt replace the keyboard as the primary input device.

Cameras. Still images and video can be captured by a camera and the image or video sequence stored in a digital file. Modern digital cameras produce images in binary form. Older analogue cameras require the image to be digitized before storage.

Output Devices

There are two main output devices: monitors and printers. Both are judged by the clarity with which they produce images and text.

Monitors. High-resolution monitors have become more desirable as the use of multi-media has increased. Flat-screen displays have also dramatically increased in resolution and size and decreased in price as the laptop market has expanded.

Printers. Hard copy of computer files is obtained on a printer. Modern printers use bubble-jet technology for cheap, good-quality printouts; and laser technology for medium-priced, high-quality print. Good quality, colour bubble-jet printout is available. High quality, colour printout is available using laser printers, although the price is still somewhat expensive for whole-scale use.

AN INFORMATION PROCESSING SYSTEM

Figure 4.7 illustrates an information system model based on the components discussed earlier.

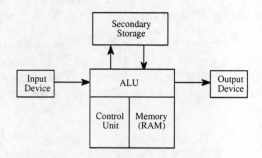

Figure 4.7. Information system model.

The system in Figure 4.7 is known as the *Von Neumann architecture*. One of the disadvantages of this architecture is that all input and output passes through the ALU so that all internal operations must cease every time a data transfer is required. However, the CPU performs calculations much faster than the input/output devices and is able to cope with both processes.

An improvement on the Von Neumann architecture was *Direct Memory Access (DMA)* as illustrated in Figure 4.8. In DMA, the control unit is still responsible for controlling the input/output operations, but the ALU is no longer responsible for data transfer. Although this alleviates the problem, it can still suffer under high transfer rates.

The use of a peripheral controller introduced full parallelism into peripheral operation. An *input/output (I/O) controller* is a special-purpose computer designed to take the responsibility and the load of input/output transfers away from the control unit.

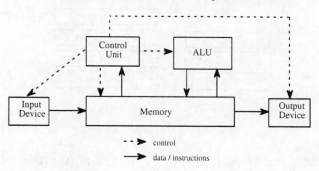

Figure 4.8. DMA system model.

COMPUTER PROGRAMS

Two types of programs (or software) run in an information processing system.

- **Operating Systems.** An *operating system*, or *system software*, looks after the operation of the computer itself.

- **Applications.** An *application* is a software program that performs a specific task such as word processing, drawing, games etc.

Operating Systems

In the 1950s and 1960s every computer program had to control the computer as well as control each specific piece of attached hardware such as tape drives, secondary storage, keyboard and printers. Software was therefore much larger than necessary to just do its function. Programs were also very specific to particular hardware and re-writing software for new hardware was a time-consuming task. In addition, running an application was very labour-intensive because the operator had to clear storage devices, load up the application and data, and run the program. These two problems of hardware dependence and operator-intensive involvement were reduced by the introduction of the *operating system (OS)* in the 1970s.

An OS is an integrated set of specialised programs that manages the resources and overall operations of a computer. Figure 4.9(a) shows the 1950s situation where each application ran directly in the hardware. Figure 4.9(b) shows the inclusion of the operating system as an interface between the application and the hardware.

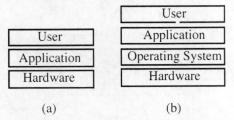

(a)   (b)

Figure 4.9. Inclusion of an OS in the computer architecture.

The user communicates with the OS, supplies applications programs and input data, and receives output results. However, the user does not usually have to know how the OS controls hardware. The OS hides these complexities from the user. Early OS examples included CP/M80 and DOS. Modern operating systems include Windows 95/98, Windows NT, OS/2, and Unix.

OS Functions

We have just seen that one of the functions of an OS is to control *input/output (I/O) housekeeping operations*. The OS monitors keyboard display, and printers and controls data movement between primary and secondary storage.

The overall management of the computer is under the control of an OS master program that is called a *supervisor, monitor,* or *kernel.* The kernel program resides in memory and coordinates all other parts of the OS. Other OS programs remain in secondary storage until the kernel calls for them.

In many PC systems, the OS kernel, other specialised OS programs, and applications programs are all stored on secondary storage. When the PC is turned on, the OS kernel is automatically loaded into primary storage in a process called *initialisation*. The remainder of the OS is then read in to memory and input/output devices are initialised. This process is called *bootstrapping*.

When the user requires an application program, the kernel consults a special file directory to determine the size of the application, and main memory is checked to see if enough space is available. If so, the kernel calls in, and then turns control over to, a specialised *basic input/output system (BIOS)* program that loads the application. Once completed, the kernel regains system control.

The OS constantly monitors the status of the computer system. It responds to user "HELP" commands and alerts the user when I/O devices need attention, when errors occur, or when other abnormal conditions arise.

Graphical User Interface (GUI)

Before leaving our discussion of operating systems, it is worth looking at the further stages in computing development. As shown in Figure 4.10(a) and (b), computing software in the 1950s and 1960s was enhanced by the incorporation of the operating system in the 1970s so that the application developer was not required to include software that controlled specific hardware. The introduction of *graphical user interfaces (GUI)* in the 1980s (Figure 4.10(c)), meant that application developers no longer had to create their own interfaces but could call on system routines to do most of the hard work like generating windows, etc.

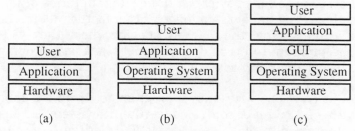

(a) (b) (c)

Figure 4.10. Introduction of GUI.

Application Software

This section discusses application software, which comprises the programs of computer instructions stored on magnetic disk, CD-ROM or other suitable storage devices. To run a program, the computer loads it from storage into main memory, from where the CPU executes the instructions. Application software tells the computer how to do the tasks required of it.

First Generation Language (Machine Code)

Some early computers input instructions to the CPU by literally *programming in binary*. Each bit of each byte was implemented as a physical ON-OFF switch on an external control. Setting eight switches OFF or ON would load up the first instruction byte, which could be entered by flicking another switch. A new eight-bit instruction would then be physically entered and so on. Because the programmer gives instructions directly to the CPU, the program is called *machine code*, or a *first-generation language*. However, you cannot imagine running any modern application in this way. Whilst other forms of entry such as magnetic tape ease the process, programming in machine code is a very difficult and error-prone task.

Second Generation Languages (Assembler)

Faster, more accurate programming became available through *assembler languages*, which are slightly more human-readable than machine code and are sometimes called *second-generation languages*. With an assembler language the programmer can write instructions in an easier form, using commands such as LDA (meaning *load accumulator*); ADC (meaning *add with carry*); and so on. The commands are called *mnemonics* or *symbolic codes*, where each code represents a number of commands that are then converted into the machine code that can be understood by the computer. Although the programmer does not need to know machine code, a good knowledge is still required of the CPU.

A further advance came through *symbolic addressing*, which expressed storage addresses in terms of symbols, rather than in terms of their absolute numeric location. Programmers no longer assign actual address numbers to symbolic data items. Now they merely specify where they want the first location in the program to be, and an assembly language program allocates locations for instructions and data.

A program of instructions written by a programmer in an assembly language is called a *source program* or *source code*. After the assembler has converted the source program into machine code, it is called an *object program* or *object code*.

Third Generation (High-level) Languages

First and second generation languages are known as *low-level* languages because they require an intimate knowledge of a particular CPU. Low-level languages are therefore machine-dependent, so that each CPU requires a different program. Coding in assembler is also time-consuming and not a natural skill. These difficulties led to the development of *third-generation languages* or *high-level languages*.

Transportability of software and ease of development have become critical issues. Therefore, most modern programs are written in high-level languages, where the programmer does not need to know the details of the CPU. For example, to add $1+1$, the programmer types a command such as $x=1+1$, which is more natural to write and much easier to document and maintain. In theory, high-level programs can run on any hardware but, in practice, some modifications are generally required to suit each platform.

Although high-level programs are more natural for humans, they cannot be understood directly by the CPU, which can only comprehend instructions in binary form. So high-level languages must be translated into machine language. With some languages, translation occurs as the program runs. This type of translation is called *interpretation*, where the system validates the program as it is entered one line at a time. If any errors are found, the programmer is prompted to rectify the error. Although this is a slow process, the main advantage of interpreted languages is that they require only small amounts of memory to run. The best-known interpreted language is BASIC, which became very popular on early microcomputers, where RAM was severely limited.

However, for most high-level languages, the program is translated *(compiled)* before it is run by using special software called a *compiler*. Again, the high-level language program is called *source code* and the compiled code is called *object code*. The compiled file is called an *executable*. In DOS, for example, these files have an extension of '.exe' or '.com'. During the compilation stage, the programmer often wants to include subroutines or functions from standard maths libraries and other libraries. This process is called *linking*.

There are many hundreds of programming languages, each with its strengths and weaknesses. A simplified lineage of the major high-level languages is presented in Figure 4.11.

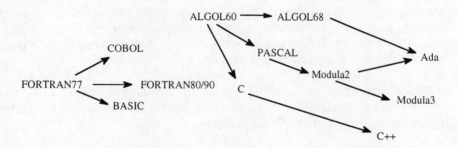

Figure 4.11. Lineage of major high-level languages.

Fourth Generation Languages (4GLs)

Fourth-generation languages (4GLs) interact with a database management system to store, manipulate and retrieve data. High-level languages are *procedural*; that is, they require the programmer to explicitly list the steps required to achieve a task. A 4GL is *non-procedural* allowing the user to specify what the output should be without specifying precisely how the result is to be achieved. The use of 4GLs is increasing but, whilst they are useful for interacting with databases, they offer less control over output and do not use hardware resources as efficiently. Most applications are therefore normally written in high-level languages.

DATABASE SYSTEMS

Early programs needed to know most of the physical characteristics of the data files they used. Programs and files were interdependent; if one was modified, the other also needed to be modified. Because they were inseparable, the data was said to be "owned" by the programs. New files needed to contain a copy of required data leading to redundancy and resulting in a waste of storage. Maintenance was difficult since changes to a piece of data were required in all affected programs. Discrepancies would inevitably arise since different applications would want to update data at different times. In addition, it was difficult to extract summary information and support enquiries. These problems were alleviated by the use of databases.

In a database, all data is merged into a single file that is shared between programs instead of belonging to any particular one. The central feature in database philosophy is the concept of data independence, which is the separation of the programmer's view of the database from knowledge of how the data is actually stored. It permits programs to have different views of the same data. A database has two levels of data independence. *Logical data independence* means that the logical structure of the data can change without having to change any of the applications. *Physical data independence* means that the layout of the data can change without affecting applications. However, total data independence is not normally possible. In practice, data independence means being able to change the data definition without having to change associated programs.

The software package that controls access to the data is called a *Database Management System (DBMS)*. Programs interact with the DBMS to retrieve, update, add or delete data. A DBMS provides:

- logical and physical data independence;
- natural organisation of data;
- data integrity, consistency, accuracy and timeliness;
- access security;
- minimisation of redundancy;
- facilities for multiple search strategies or access paths through the data;
- centralised control, usually in the form of a Database Administrator;
- concurrent access by a number of programs; and
- ad hoc enquiry, without the need for special programs.

Logical and physical data independence requires three levels of data description:

- A chart of the physical layout of the data on the storage devices.
- A chart of the entire logical database (called a *schema*).
- Charts of those portions of the data that are oriented to the needs of the individual applications (called *sub-schemas*).

Databases are administered by a Database Administrator, who has a number of responsibilities:

- creation and modification of the database description and physical organisation;
- granting users access to database areas; and
- making back-up copies of the database and repair of damage.

Data Models

A DBMS uses a *data model* to organise and retrieve data. There are three basic types of data model: *hierarchical*, *network* and *relational*.

Let us first look at the simple file structure shown in Figure 4.12. A *file* is a set of cards, each card being a *record* containing a number of *fields*. In a database, a record is also called an *entity* such as a part, manufacturer, person, or company.

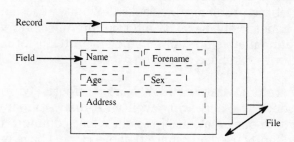

Figure 4.12. A simple file structure.

A *relationship* is a logical connection between two or more entities, such as the fact that JONES belongs to the MARKETING department. This simple structure is sufficient for most business problems. Structures that are more complex require *data abstraction*, which is beyond the scope of this book.

Both entities and relationships can be considered facts known by the database system. Entities are straightforward and are represented in all three models as *files*. The associated pieces of information within an entity are *fields* in a file. Relationships, or the other hand, are represented differently by each model.

Relationships may be one-to-one, many-to-one, or many-to-many. A many-to-one relationship is the most common, such as the relationship between person and company. A single company may employ several people, but a person normally belongs to only one company. An example of a many-to-many relationship would be the relationship between students and courses. A single student would be enrolled in several courses and a single course usually contains many students. Relationships may also involve more than two entities, as the relationship between parts, suppliers and projects. A single supplier may supply many parts to many projects, or conversely, a single project may have many parts supplied by many suppliers.

As the relationships between the data increase in number, the database becomes very complex. The method that the DBMS uses to represent the relationships and to manipulate the data affects the productivity of the end user.

Hierarchical Data Model

The oldest of the data models is the hierarchical model, which has a straightforward representation of relationships between entities. Data is organised as in a hierarchical paper list. Searching the database can only be performed efficiently from top to bottom. The user must specify at the design stage how the data is to be accessed. So, the hierarchical model works very well for some database problems, but lacks flexibility. The hierarchical model can also be space-inefficient because information must be repeated in many records. Data redundancy is not only inefficient in terms of storage, but also creates problems with database consistency.

Whilst the hierarchical data model works effectively for many-to-one relationships, it does not cope very well with many-to-many relationships. Because the many-to-one relationship is the most common, the hierarchical data model is frequently used and more flexible models have evolved.

Network Model

The network model solves the problems of data-redundancy and of many-to-many relationships. Each entity is represented as an independent file and the relationships between files are represented by links. The network model therefore has the advantage that redundant data is not stored and data can be accessed efficiently in many different ways.

Although the network model is a vast improvement over the hierarchical model, there are several disadvantages. First, it is very difficult to modify the database because there is a tight binding between files and relationships (links are specified when the database is designed and cannot be changed easily). The second major disadvantage is that the user must specify link names when querying the database, which makes navigating the database complex and data-dependent. The relational model solves these remaining difficulties.

Relational Model

Simply, a relational system:

- is made up of only flat files (such as tables);
- allows the user to pick any fields from any file for data manipulation (*project operator*);
- allows the user to select any set of records for manipulation, subject to some condition (*select operator*); and
- allows two or more files to be joined into one logical file where fields from records in each file match (*join operator*).

The *select*, *project*, and *join* operators are mathematical terms used to define the operators of the relational model. Select constructs a new block by taking a horizontal sub-set of an existing table, that is, all the rows that satisfy a particular condition. Project constructs a new table by taking a vertical sub-set of an existing table by extracting specified columns. The join operator constructs a new table by taking two tables that have a column defined over the same domain and taking the rows that have the same value in that column. Complex questions can be answered by using combinations of the select, project, and join operators.

The advantage of the relational model is that relationships are stored simply as another entity in the database – as a two-dimensional file with fields. The link between the entities is logical, not physical, allowing much greater freedom to modify the database. The database may be designed slowly, one file at a time, or modified to change with a changing environment.

Another major advantage of the relational model is that the user need not specify the most efficient path to find the data. The user specifies that the files be joined and the job of deciding how best to perform the join is left to the DBMS.

Database Redundancy

There are two main sorts of database redundancy. A *replicated database* stores copies of all its data elements at every location where the database exists. Keeping a replicated database up-to-date is relatively straightforward: each location receives a copy of any change of the data. If a database is not currently available, the change must be re-issued when the site becomes available. Because each change must be transmitted to each site, replicated databases normally have a high communications requirement.

In a *distributed database*, data elements are distributed between the various locations where the database exists. The storage structure is segmented such that each segment, while logically associated with others, is stored on physically separate storage. Segments can then be allocated to localities where they are most likely to be used, so that local processing is maintained and overall communications reduced without sacrificing the benefits of data integration. A distributed database may also include some replication.

SUMMARY

We have now addressed most of the components of communication and information systems. In the next chapter, we discuss networking, through which information systems are connected together.

5.
Networking Fundamentals

This chapter deals with networking. We look first at the local area networks (LANs) that connect a number of computer devices within a small area, normally confined by an office or a building. We then discuss networks that interconnect buildings (that is, interconnect LANs), called metropolitan area networks (MANs) or campus networks. Normally, a MAN is geographically confined to a group of buildings with a common purpose such as a university campus, a factory or a defence base. MANs (or LANs) can be interconnected by wide area networks (WANs), which normally extend across a city, between cities, or worldwide. Generally, LANs, MANs and WANs are based on different network technologies. However, as we will see, the distinction between WAN, MAN and LAN has become blurred as the various technologies converge. LAN technologies are now normally called *networking* technologies and the interconnection of LANs is called *internetworking*.

First, however, we need to understand a reference model that is used to describe the way in which information systems communicate.

ISO OSI 7-LAYER REFERENCE MODEL

Most digital communication systems use procedures arranged in accordance with the International Standards Organisation (ISO) Open Systems Interconnection (OSI) Reference Model which defines seven layers or levels as illustrated in Figure 5.1. The procedures used at each layer are called protocols.

Throughout the Reference Model, each layer is transparent to the layer above. This is achieved by each layer receiving a block of information from the layer above and then adding the information needed for its protocol. At the receiving end, each layer receives a block from the layer below it, strips off the information required for its protocol and passes the resultant information up to the next layer.

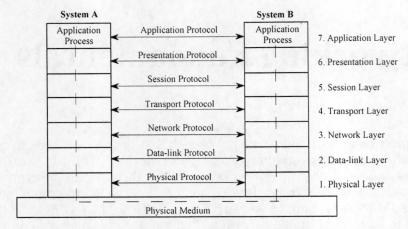

Figure 5.1. Protocol layers for the ISO OSI Reference Model.

The seven layers are summarised below.

Layer 1. The Physical Layer allows the connection, maintenance and disconnection of physical circuits between different types of devices. It provides the mechanical, electrical, functional and procedural characteristics that enable data to be sent from one terminal to another. This is basic electrical communication that covers the standards associated with plugs, sockets, leads etc. Examples are RS-232, RS-449, V.21, V.24 and X.21.

Layer 2. The Data Link Layer allows point-to-point or node-to-node control. It is often called the frame level because it specifies the formats in which transmissions are embedded in frames. It incorporates error detection and correction and data-flow control.

Layer 3. The Network Layer controls the exchange of data so that the network is transparent to the data. Routing, flow control and switching are provided at this layer. X.25 is an example of a network protocol.

Layer 4. The Transport Layer establishes and terminates connections between devices, and provides error handling and flow control.

Layer 5. The Session Layer determines the rules for establishing and ending a communication and re-establishing a connection if it is interrupted. It determines the right of a device to interrupt another, checks for user authenticity and keeps track of billing details.

Layer 6. The Presentation Layer provides code conversion, compression and standard layouts for devices and peripherals. The layer's main job is to ensure that the data is 'presented' to the Application Layer in a way that layer can understand.

Layer 7. The final Application Layer is responsible for implementing the tasks to be performed for a user to run an application.

Layers 1 to 3 contain the network protocols. Layers 4 and above contain the user-to-user protocols in which the network takes no part. The network protocols are obviously the most important from a communications point of view.

LAN STANDARDS

LAN standards are defined by the IEEE 802 committee, which has produced a number of standards over recent years. When the IEEE 802 committees were implementing the bottom two layers of the ISO Model, they divided Layer 2, the Data Link Layer, into two functions: *Logical Link Control (LLC)* and *Media Access Control (MAC)*. Figure 5.2 illustrates the relationship of the IEEE 802 structure to the bottom two layers of the ISO Model.

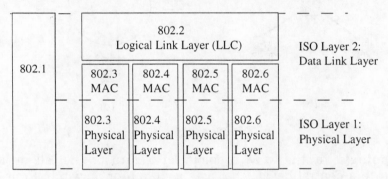

Figure 5.2. IEEE LAN Standards and the ISO Reference Model.

The following IEEE standards are defined:

- **IEEE 802.1** defines the 802 family of standards.
- **IEEE 802.2** defines the Logical Link Control Standard.
- **IEEE 802.3** a bus topology using CSMA/CD.
- **IEEE 802.4** a bus topology using token passing.
- **IEEE 802.5** a ring topology using token passing.
- **IEEE 802.6** dual bus topology using fibre optics.

LAN TOPOLOGIES

The way in which the devices on a local area network are connected together is called the *topology*. There are three main types: *bus*, *star* and *ring*.

Bus Topology. In the most straightforward LAN topology, devices are connected to a common linear transmission medium called a *bus* as illustrated in Figure 5.3(a). All devices are attached to the bus providing a simple, economical method of interconnecting devices. A failure in any one device will not affect the rest, but a single point of failure on the bus will cause the entire network to fail.

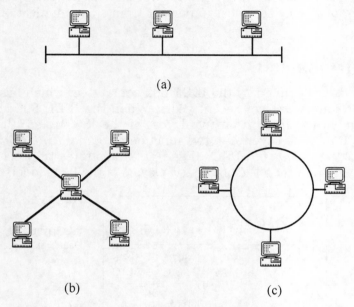

(a)

(b)   (c)

Figure 5.3. LAN topologies.

Star Topology. In the *star* topology of Figure 5.3(b), all devices are connected to a central device that acts as a hub or a switch. Considerable redundancy is gained since a single point of network failure will only affect the single device connected on that cable.

Ring Topology. In a *ring* topology, shown in Figure 5.3(c), devices are connected in a circular fashion so that data is passed around the network from one device to the next, until it returns to the transmitting device. The topology is vulnerable to both device failure and a single point of network failure.

Logical versus Physical Topology. As we will see shortly, LAN topologies are not as simple as the above physical descriptions imply. Often a LAN technique uses a certain logical topology (that is the information will travel in accordance with one of the above topologies) but the LAN will be wired physically to look like another topology. The most common examples are networks that are either a logical bus or ring, but are wired to be a physical star topology.

NETWORK DEVICES

A LAN will normally comprise the following elements.

Network Server. A *network server* (more traditionally called a *file server*) is a fast processor with large storage and memory capacity. It manages the network and the network file system and provides a number of functions such as: printers, disk space, applications, back-up storage and the network operating system.

Network Operating System (NOS). The NOS is the network's central software which runs on the server and provides the basis for resource sharing by the other devices on the network. The NOS normally provides: file and print sharing; support for multi-user applications; electronic mail; and security procedures. Examples of NOSes include UNIX, Novell NetWare, Banyan Vines, LAN Manager and Windows NT and to a lesser extent Windows 95.

Devices. LAN devices are generally based on a processor and access the network through the network interface card discussed below. The type of network devices can vary from printers and disk drives through to PCs of differing processing powers and to mainframe computers. Each device communicates with other devices and with the server through the common infrastructure of the network. The major devices on a LAN are workstations such as PCs. Each workstation operates its own operating system such as Windows 95 and also runs a shell program that allows it to communicate with the server and other devices on the network. The selection of the type of workstation will depend on the function required of the device.

Network Interface Cards (NICs). NICs provide the interface between the network device (the PC, for example) and the network. Different cards are required depending on the media access technique, such as Ethernet or Token Ring. Different cards are also required for each type of network device. Similarly, the NIC must support the required physical medium of the LAN. Most modern NICs support more than one physical medium. NICs also provide support for network management devices on the network and can provide information on the device's performance and availability. NICs are also commonly called *network cards* or *LAN cards*.

LAN MEDIA

The *LAN medium* is the physical transmission medium used to connect devices. LAN media are traditionally cable-based but, as we will see shortly, wireless links are also available. We have already discussed each of the media types in Chapter 2, but the following sections will discuss how the various media are used in LANs.

Coaxial Cable. Coaxial cable is used in Ethernet LANs: thick (10mm) coaxial cable (RG-11); and thin (5mm) coaxial cable (RG-58). RG-11 has a minimum bend radius of 25cm and RG-58 has a minimum bend radius of 5cm. Thick coax has better attenuation properties, but is more difficult to install and connect as its bend radius is not suitable for cabling inside rooms and must be installed in ceilings or under-floor ducts.

Twisted Pair Cable. Twisted pair is a popular LAN medium due to its light weight, low cost and ease of deployment. Both unshielded twisted pair (UTP) and shielded twisted pair (STP) are used. Twisted pair is graded from Level 1 to Level 5 (often called Category 1 to Category 5).

Fibre Optic Cable. Fibre optic cables can be used for all elements of a LAN. More, commonly, however, fibre is used in the backbone and twisted pair or coaxial cable is used to connect devices. This takes advantage of both media: fibre optics provide the high capacity for the backbone; and twisted pair provide the light weight and ease of termination required for each workstation.

Wireless Networks. Wireless networks use electromagnetic radiation as the medium; either in the RF or infra-red band. Wireless LANs are also sometimes called cableless LANs or CLANs. The use of radio or infra-red frequencies does not affect the LAN topology although a different interface method is obviously required. Wireless LANs are attractive to network designers and users as the devices have much greater flexibility in temporary and permanent re-deployment.

- **RF.** The use of radio frequencies is restricted by the problems of finding sufficient frequencies to be allocated to the technology. The radio frequency spectrum is already over-crowded and potentially many LANs would wish to use the technology. Whilst the use of low powers may help with frequency re-use, the deployment of terminals is constrained. Performance of RF networks can be enhanced by spread-spectrum technology.

- **Infra-red.** Infra-red networks have higher bandwidths than radio frequencies and do not have the same frequency allocation problems. They have the disadvantage, however, of requiring line-of-sight transmission from one device to another.

MEDIA ACCESS TECHNIQUES

Media access techniques allow the devices on the LAN to gain access to the shared media. All devices cannot access the LAN simultaneously; there must be some protocol by which an orderly, timely access is available to all devices.

There are two main types of signalling used in LANs: *baseband* and *broadband*. Baseband systems are generally digital, operate at speeds of 10Mbps and use 50Ω cable. Broadband systems are analogue, operate at speeds of around 50Mbps and use 75Ω cable. Each system uses different connection methods. Broadband systems utilise FDM to provide multiple carriers to obtain higher throughput, and are able to serve a very large number of devices. Broadband systems are more complex than baseband systems and are therefore more expensive. Their capacity advantage over baseband is further reduced by the fact that large baseband networks can be provided through the use of bridges and routers.

There are two main baseband protocols employed: *carrier sense multiple access/collision detect (CSMA/CD)* and *token passing*. Each is discussed below by examining the two main techniques that utilise the protocols (Ethernet and Token Ring, respectively). Ethernet and Token Ring account for approximately 95% of the installed networks.

Ethernet

Carrier Sense Multiple Access / Collision Detect (CSMA/CD)

The CSMA/CD protocol allows *multiple access* to a LAN. *Carrier sense* refers to the way in which a device that wants to transmit checks the LAN for a signal to see if any other device on the network is transmitting data. If the LAN is busy, the device will wait until the other device is finished. When no signal is present on the LAN, the device can transmit.

A problem will still occur, however, if two devices simultaneously check that the network is quiet and decide to transmit data. If that happens, the data arriving at the receiving station will be corrupted. So a protocol is required to prevent transmissions in those circumstances. *Collision detect (CD)* requires a transmitting device to monitor the LAN while it is transmitting. If the device detects a collision, it will stop transmitting, wait a pre-determined, random time and then sense the LAN before attempting to re-transmit.

Ethernet runs at 10Mbps although it only has an effective throughput of 3Mbps.

Ethernet Media

The following format is to describe Ethernet and IEEE802.3 media:

Speed - Transmission Type - Segment Length

where speed is in MHz, transmission type is baseband or broadband, and segment length is the maximum length of segment in multiples of 100m. Examples include: 10Base5 - thick coaxial cable (RJ11); 10Base2 - thin coaxial cable (RJ58); 10BaseT - UTP or STP; and10BaseF - fibre optic cable.

Ethernet Configurations

Ethernet operates in the baseband mode and uses a bus topology. The bus is terminated with terminating resistors (50Ω for baseband systems) to avoid unwanted reflections on the transmission line. As illustrated in Figure 5.4(a), the distance between terminating resistors is called a *segment*. More commonly, the resistors are not shown but replaced by a vertical line as shown in Figure 5.4(b).

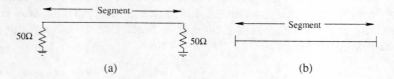

(a)   (b)

Figure 5.4. Ethernet segment.

The maximum segment length will depend on the type of LAN medium used. Maximum lengths are: 10Base5 - 500m, 10Base2 - 185m and 10BaseT - 100m. If longer lengths are required, segments can be joined with repeaters as shown in Figure 5.5. The repeater re-times and re-generates a signal from one segment to another. Regardless of the medium used, a maximum number of five segments can be joined in series (that is, a maximum of four repeaters can be used).

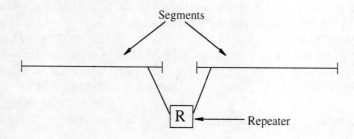

Figure 5.5. Two segments joined with a repeater.

Token Ring

The *token passing* media access method is more orderly than CSMA/CD. Access control is provided by a small frame of data called a *token* which circulates around the LAN until a device that wishes to transmit and takes the token and transmits a data frame in its place. Each device on the LAN looks at the data frame to see if it is the addressee. If so, it copies the frame, and lets it past once it has changed the Frame Status field to signify that the frame has been copied. Finally the frame arrives back at the originating device, which can check if the receiving device has copied the frame by checking the Frame Status field. The originating device then releases the token to signify that the LAN is idle. At any moment, therefore, either a token or a data frame is travelling around the LAN.

It should be noted that Token Ring, as its name implies, requires a logical ring network. However, for ease of maintenance and movement of devices, the cabling is actually physically star-wired as shown in Figure 5.6. The central hubs in the physical star are called *multi-station access units (MSAU)*. Each device is connected to a simplex transmission path and always transmits around the ring in the same direction.

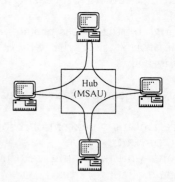

Figure 5.6. Star-wired Token Ring network.

Token ring networks run at 4Mbps or 16Mbps. Shielded or unshielded twisted pair is used. Up to 260 stations can be connected on STP and 72 on UTP.

Token Ring versus Ethernet

The comparison of Ethernet running at 10Mbps and Token Ring running at either 4Mbps or 16Mbps is not straightforward. Some major points are outlined below.

Ethernet is cheaper than Token Ring but is less reliable. Token Ring provides an orderly access technique while Ethernet is far less orderly. Token Ring has higher overheads at low levels of traffic but is better under a heavy workload than Ethernet. Token Ring is therefore better at transferring large files, particularly on a busy LAN.

In summary, the differences are hard to quantify. Ethernet is generally preferred if the network will be operating at a medium workload. If a heavy workload is expected, Token Ring is preferred.

ADVANTAGES AND DISADVANTAGES OF LANS

Advantages. The primary advantages of LANs are:

- replacement of multiple point-to-point networks;
- better information management through improved accessibility and reduced duplication;
- improved productivity through automation of routine functions;
- improved communication between personnel;
- reduction of costs through sharing expensive resources such as storage, printers, modems, back-up devices etc;
- allows cooperative and distributive processing between PCs and servers and hosts;
- improved security through better access procedures; and
- each user has only one workstation with which to access multiple hosts, applications and peripherals.

Disadvantages. LANs may have some disadvantages:

- possible higher cost (depending on extent of resource sharing);
- increased training requirement;
- increased management and planning required (possibly requiring additional personnel); and
- application development becomes more complex.

INTERNETWORKING

LANs connect a number of devices together in a small geographic area. Often, the devices will want to communicate to other devices that are not collocated and are often on another LAN in another area. The interconnection of LANs is called *internetworking*.

Figure 5.7 shows two networks, LAN A and LAN B. There are four devices that can be used to interconnect these networks: *repeater*, *bridge*, *router*, and *gateway*. These devices operate at different levels of the OSI reference model. They are illustrated in Figure 5.7 and discussed in more detail below.

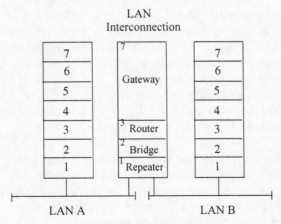

Figure 5.7. Network interconnection.

Repeaters

We have already met the repeater as a device that operates at Layer 1 and simply re-times and regenerates the signal to transfer data from a network of one type to a network of the same type. As we saw earlier, a repeater is the device used to interconnect Ethernet segments or to interconnect Token Ring LANs. It would not be used to connect an Ethernet LAN to a Token Ring LAN. For this to be possible a higher level of translation must occur.

Bridges

A bridge is slightly more intelligent than a repeater, but only just. Bridges operate at the MAC sub-layer (Layer 2) and therefore can only interconnect LANs of the same type. Bridges read the destination and source addresses in the packets or frames and forward them on to another LAN depending on the address.

A MAC layer bridge has a high throughput due to the low level of intelligence required to interconnect two LANs. When a bridge receives frames, it examines the source address and begins to build a table of addresses on each of the segments to which it is connected. As each frame is received from one segment, the bridge examines the addresses for the other segment and makes the following simple decisions:

- if it knows of the address on the outgoing side, the frame is forwarded to that segment;
- if the address is on the incoming side, the frame is discarded; or
- if the frame is not in its address, the bridge forwards the frame on.

As soon as all devices have transmitted, the bridge will know on which segment they are connected. These simple rules mean that the bridge acts as a filter, only sending frames onto a segment if they are destined for a device on that segment. On Ethernet LANs this is a very desirable feature since the segments can effectively operate as independent LANs until frames need to be sent from one to another. This reduces the potential collisions on each segment and, unlike repeaters, allows the design rules for the maximum number of segments to begin again. A bridge could therefore be used to join two maximum-length Ethernet segments.

Bridges provide high-speed interconnection devices, ideal to interconnect similar networks where protocol conversion is not necessary. Bridges can be used to restrict traffic on the network to certain segments, and to keep unwanted traffic off the network backbone. However, these attributes mean that bridges are significantly slower than repeaters.

Advantages of Bridges. The use of bridges has a number of advantages:

• The physical size can be extended beyond the normal maximum design limitation since each network on either side of the bridge can be of maximum length.
• The volume of traffic on the LAN is reduced as the bridge restricts traffic to the appropriate side.
• LAN managers can restrict access by controlling address lists in the bridge to prevent selected traffic from leaving one network and appearing on the other.

Still, bridges have only limited intelligence and have their greatest use in connecting similar networks together to alleviate design constraints in allowable maximum lengths of network. Better network connectivity can only be provided with more intelligent devices.

Routers

The next level of connectivity of networks is provided by *routers*, which are Layer 3 (Network Layer) devices. Routers link LANs that are using different MAC protocols such as Ethernet and Token Ring but they need a common network protocol such as TCP/IP. Applications address data to a router that either forwards it to another router on another network or passes it on for delivery to its local network. Routers contain a considerable degree of intelligence and have knowledge of the network. If the data is not destined for its local network, the router determines the best path to its destination and selects the appropriate router on to which to forward the data.

Routers are configurable, multi-port devices that forward data based on network information and the destination address. The router configuration can be controlled by the network manager to route traffic by different routes depending on a number of parameters such as priority, required response time, or cheapest path. Unlike bridges that extend networks, routers are used to interconnect LANs and to segment a larger network rather than forming one. Additionally, because of the additional processing, routers are much slower than bridges and require a portion of the network bandwidth to communicate amongst themselves.

Routers provide similar filtering and bridging functions as bridges, but they offer more sophisticated capabilities such as network management and the ability to share network information with each other using routing protocols running at Layer 3. They also offer limited security at this low level through the ability to control access lists and protocols.

Selecting the best route between source and destination is achieved by routing algorithms that contain complex rules to take into account a variety of network factors. There are two types of algorithm: *static routing* and *dynamic routing*. Static routing requires the network administrator to manually configure the routing table of each router in the network. Because of the effort required, static routing is normally only used in small networks. Dynamic routing involves the use of intelligent routers that can re-configure themselves to account for failed or congested links. The routers can be given an initial configuration or can start with no knowledge of the network and create a routing table by observing the network.

Gateways

Two completely different networks can be connected by a *gateway*. A gateway operates at Layer 7 (the Application Layer) and translates between two different protocol stacks. The gateway runs both protocol stacks - corresponding to the two stacks in the two disparate networks being connected. As illustrated in Figure 5.8, LAN A operates with one protocol stack, which can be understood by the gateway since it operates on that LAN with a similar stack. The gateway can also understand the protocol stack employed by LAN B since it also operates on that network. At Layer 7, the gateway can be considered to be a translator between host machines on the two networks. In addition to protocol conversion, gateways route data and therefore they are by far the slowest interconnection device. However, if protocol conversion is required, this lower speed is normally accepted gladly as the cost of performing protocol conversion in each device is prohibitive and a gateway can perform the translation on behalf of a complete LAN. A common LAN-WAN gateway converts Ethernet to X.25.

Battlefield Command Systems

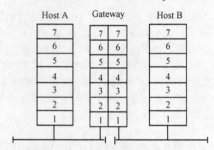

Figure 5.8. Gateway operation.

Comparison of Internetworking Devices

Table 5.1 provides a brief comparison of internetworking devices.

FEATURE	REPEATER	BRIDGE	ROUTER	GATEWAY
Layer of Operation	1	2	3	7
Purpose	Connects segments of same network type	Extends and connects networks of same type	Interconnects different networks	Interconnects different networks with different hosts
Protocol Conversion	No	No	Yes	Yes
Intelligence	No	Very limited	Yes	Yes
Speed	Very fast	Fast	Slower	Slower still
Network Management Support	No	No	Yes	Yes
Security Features	No	No	Limited (Access Control)	Yes

Table 5.1. A comparison of internetworking devices.

Internetworking Protocols

Communications between two internetworking devices are controlled by an appropriate internetworking protocol. At the Data Link Layer (Layer 2) the most common protocol is the ITU's High-level Data Link Control (HDLC) standard or versions of it. The most important Layer 3, or Network Layer protocols are discussed in the following sections.

X.25

X.25 is an ITU packet switching interface standard that defines the interface between a device and a packet switching network. The standard was first issued in 1976 and has been revised a number of times since. As a supplement to X.25, ITU developed a set of standards defining packet assembly and disassembly so that the network can interconnect different terminal types with different abilities to accommodate all protocol layers. The packet assemble/disassemble (PAD) facility is defined by three standards as illustrated in Figure 5.9:

- X.3 - describes the PAD functions and its control parameters.
- X.28 - describes the protocol between a terminal and the PAD.
- X.29 - describes the protocol between the PAD and a host computer.

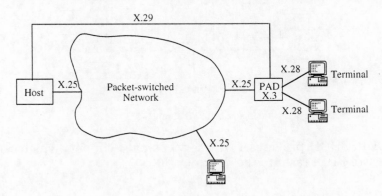

Figure 5.9. PAD protocols.

Point-to-Point Protocol (PPP)

PPP is a lower-level Internet standard used to configure and manage communication links between remote multi-protocol routers. It was approved by the Internet Engineering Task Force (IETF) in 1989 as a draft standard for TCP/IP serial communications to improve the existing standard Serial Line Interface Protocol (SLIP). PPP improved on SLIP by providing the ability to transmit packets between routers using multiple protocols such as TCP/IP, OSI, AppleTalk etc. The encapsulation of these different protocols into PPP is defined by the IETF standard. PPP provides true point-to-point communications between routers allowing them to exchange addresses and to compress and encrypt data.

Fibre Distributed Data Interface (FDDI)

FDDI is a timed token passing network over fibre optic cable and UTP. The standard defines a network that operates at speeds of 100Mbps with a maximum perimeter length of 200km with nodes no less than 2km apart. The maximum number of nodes is 1,000.

As illustrated in Figure 5.10, the network topology is based on a dual ring to which devices connect either as a single device or as a wiring concentrator. Class A devices connect to both the *primary* and the *secondary rings*, whilst Class B devices are only connected to the primary ring through a wiring concentrator. Class A devices may use both rings simultaneously giving an effective data rate of 200Mbps. Cable breaks can be addressed by rapid re-configuration of the dual ring into a single ring until the fault is repaired.

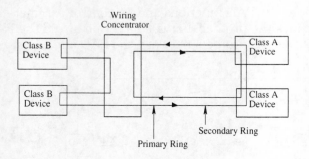

Figure 5.10. FDDI topology.

Copper DDI (CDDI) provides FDDI services over copper, which will allows the delivery of FDDI rates to the desktop.

Frame Relay

Frame Relay was developed for use in the ISDN environment and uses a shared public network to appear as a point-to-point connection. It uses a stream-lined data link protocol to provide link layer switching and multiplexing over low-error, high-speed digital links. Its data throughput is higher than other internetworking protocols due to reduced error correction procedures on the assumption that the digital circuit will be relatively error-free.

Frame Relay is based on a modified version of the Link Access Protocol for D Channel (LAPD) and envelopes data packets or frames, adapting the envelope size to fit the frame. An address is then added containing an explicit route as well as content and handling-priority information. This allows the transmission of traffic without the delays associated with store and forward and re-addressing.

SWITCHING TECHNIQUES

A communications network provides connections between each of its users. There are four main techniques for establishing such connections: *circuit switching, message switching, packet switching,* and *cell switching.*

Circuit Switching

A *circuit* is a two-way path for carrying information in either digital or analogue form. In the most extreme case a circuit would be permanently established between any two users who require to converse or transfer information. This is very inefficient since it would require a large number of circuits, some of which will be used heavily and some may not be used at all. A much more efficient use of resources is available using *circuit switching* where each user is connected to a central *switch* that is able to interconnect any two users. A simple example is illustrated in Figure 5.11. A circuit is established between two users at the demand of one of those users. The path exists only for the duration of the call.

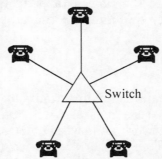

Figure 5.11. A simple switched network with one switch.

Figure 5.12 shows how the circuit switched network is built up. Users are connected to a switch, and switches are interconnected using *trunk* links. The terminology was developed in the commercial network, based on a tree (since the structure was very similar). Major links between switches were *trunk links* and links from switches to users were called *branch lines*. Switches were called Public Access Branch Exchanges (PABX). Additional trunk lines then interconnect each suburban PABX with a major switch in the city and these major switches are again interconnected by high capacity trunk links between cities.

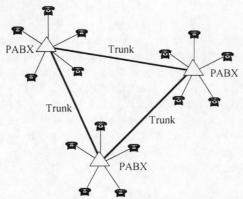

Figure 5.12. Interconnection of PABX using trunk links.

The advantage of circuit switching is that, once the circuit has been set up, there are no delays and communication between the two ends can continue until the circuit is disconnected. Circuit switching is the most efficient switching technique for voice communications since real-time conversations generally require a circuit for the duration of the conversation.

Circuit switching is a very efficient way of transferring large volumes of data between data terminals and has the added advantage of requiring relatively simple protocols. However, circuit switching has significant disadvantages for data transfer since it makes poor utilisation of links and equipment and is generally expensive to implement. Additionally, the set up and clear down times are long compared to the time it takes to transmit the data and the user must continually retry to connect if the other subscriber is absent or engaged.

Message Switching

A *message* is a discrete data communication. Message switching is a *store-and-forward* concept where a message with an appropriate destination address is sent into the network and switched at each network node until it reaches its destination. The network switches (often called *store-and-forward switches*) can accommodate links that are congested or unavailable by storing messages at the node or by sending them via an alternative route. For multiple addresses, switches make copies of the message to be forwarded to each destination.

Message switching has an advantage over circuit switching in that it makes good use of the available links and equipment. It does, however, have long response times since messages are stored awaiting available links. Although this is acceptable for traffic for human consumption, the types of delay experienced make message switching unsuited to data communications.

Packet Switching

Packet switching combines the response of circuit switching and the efficient link utilisation of message switching by imposing a maximum length on the transmitted messages. Messages are split into packets (typically 128 bytes long) so that a system of time division multiplexing is forced onto the network and long messages do not cause blockages. Packet switching is an economical and cost-effective technique for passing data, as the time-division interleaving provides automatic adjustment of the network according to demand. There are three types of packet-switched network: *datagram networks*; *virtual-circuit (VC) networks*; and *hybrid networks*.

Datagram Networks

In a datagram network, the sending terminal breaks the data up into packets that are routed individually through the network as illustrated in Figure 5.13. The receiving terminal reconstructs the original message from the packets arriving in random order. A datagram network is very rugged. If a link fails while the data is being transmitted, then the network will dynamically re-route any packets still in transit around the damaged part of the network.

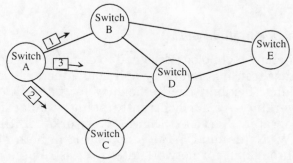

Figure 5.13. Datagram network in packet switching.

The main disadvantage of datagram networks is that every packet must have associated with it a lengthy header containing enough information for the packet to be switched to its destination. This represents an overhead of approximately 15%, which most private network providers find unacceptable and therefore tend to choose the virtual-circuit approach.

Virtual-circuit (VC) Networks

A VC is a notional connection between two terminals using a fixed route across the network as illustrated in Figure 5.14. Since packets on a VC are maintained in the order in which they entered, they do not require re-ordering at the receiving terminal.

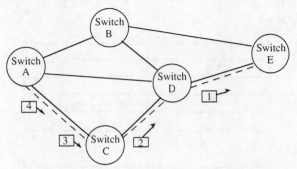

Figure 5.14. Virtual Circuit packet switching.

A Hybrid Network

A data network can be arranged to provide a combination of VCs and datagrams where a virtual circuit philosophy is supported from the outside but the network uses datagrams internally. The hybrid system has a simple interface and has the flexibility and ruggedness of a datagram network without having to insist that subscribers have a complex terminal.

Cell Switching

Asynchronous Transfer Mode (ATM)

ATM is a cell-switching technology designed to combine the benefits of circuit switching (constant transmission delay and guaranteed capacity) with those of packet switching (flexibility and efficiency for intermittent traffic). For wide area networking, ATM is currently being standardised for use in Broadband Integrated Services Digital Networks (BISDN). Although developed with WANs in mind, ATM is appearing in both MANs and LANs due to its high throughput for network-intensive distributed applications, its improved scalability and its support for many different formats such as data, voice, image and video.

ATM's use of small, fixed-length cells offers several important advantages: Because the cell headers are uniform, cell-switching can be executed in hardware, allowing greater switching speeds, and delay variability is more tightly bounded because fixed-length cells have a predictable service rate. Additionally, bandwidth reservation is easier. However, network scalability is perhaps ATM's most desirable feature. The bandwidth available to a particular user can also be increased dynamically allowing bandwidth to be provided on-demand for a particular transaction or length of time.

Interestingly, ATM's great promise is provided by its simplicity. Information is re-formatted into a standard-size 53-byte cell for transmission across the network. The cell, illustrated in Figure 5.15, contains 48 bytes of information and 5 bytes of header.

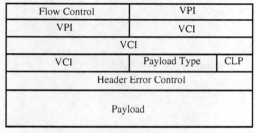

Figure 5.15. The ATM Cell.

Generic Flow Control. A four bit field for flow control.

Virtual Circuits. ATM employs a two-tier virtual circuit scheme to establish end-to-end connections. Virtual Path Identifier (VPI) is a group of virtual channels that have the same end points and the same quality of service requirements. Each VPI is sub-divided further by using Virtual Channel Identifier (VCI) number, which specifies a virtual channel between two points connected by a VPI. The virtual circuit technique reduces the amount of addressing information required in each ATM cell.

Payload Type. This field specifies the type of information carried in the information field. Different types of information carried in the cell may require different processing at the network nodes or the end user nodes.

Cell Loss Priority. This field specifies when a cell may be discarded by the network in case of congestion. The end user nodes set a bit in this field to signify if the application will allow the network to discard the cell.

Error Detection. ATM has been designed with future transmission facilities in mind, where transmission will be virtually error free. For this reason, ATM only provides error detection in the header.

SUMMARY

That completes our discussion of the fundamentals of communications and information systems. The final two chapters build on these basics to discuss the tactical communications and battlefield information systems. First, the next chapter addresses tactical communications systems, including electronic warfare systems.

6.
Battlefield Communication Systems

The pace and intensity of modern warfare requires that commanders and staffs are supported by flexible, mobile, reliable communication systems that provide sufficient capacity to cope with increasingly high traffic loads. Battlefield communications systems have a similar form in all modern armies. To understand such systems and to plan effectively for their future development, it is important to understand how they have developed and why they exist in their current form.

This chapter begins with a brief overview of the development of battlefield communication systems from early couriers to the high-capacity data networks deployed on the modern battlefield. It then describes the characteristics of battlefield communications, and the Combat Net Radio and Trunk Communications Sub-systems are described in some detail.

A BRIEF HISTORY

In early armies, communications were provided by courier or dispatch rider, who passed messages from the commander to his subordinates. Although the means of transport has changed considerably over the years, dispatch riders still provide a very valuable service in transmitting bulky information around the battlefield. Several types of information such as map overlays and photographs cannot be passed efficiently over many communications links. Other information does not need to be transmitted urgently and can therefore be passed by hand, freeing communications links for more urgent traffic.

Over the years, large scale use has also been made of visual signalling with the Romans, Incans and Persians providing networks of beacons along main roads. Early armies often used smoke and fire signals, coloured flags and other devices. Although transmission times were reduced by the invention of the telescope in the early seventeenth century, there was little real development in battlefield communication techniques until military communications requirements began to expand as fronts became wider, weapons became more sophisticated, and logistic tails became longer. To attack successfully, to deploy reinforcements, to commit reserves and to ward off counterattacks, commanders had to be informed instantly of events on distant battlefields - more swiftly than was possible by courier.

The Electric Telegraph and Telephone

The first military use of the electric telegraph was during the Crimean War (1853-56), where it was used tactically and strategically, with a submarine cable laid from Varna to Balaclava. In 1859, the electric telegraph was used by the Spanish during their war with Morocco and by the French during the Franco-Austrian war. In these campaigns, both civilian equipment and civilian operators were used. In 1860, the Italian Army made use, for the first time, of purpose-built military telegraph equipment and military operators. During the American Civil War, both armies made use of electric telegraphy.

Telegraphy was the major means of communication during World War I and by the end of the war, tens of thousands of kilometres of cable had been laid by all sides. Most lines were laid as earth circuits; that is, they were single wires that used the earth as the return path for the current. Wherever possible, these wires were normally laid below the surface to protect them from the effects of artillery. To cope with the large number of buried cables, communicators developed a systematic method of laying based on a grid system of main arteries into which units and formations could connect. Each divisional area had a main artery with switching and testing centres, each of which was connected to the main arteries of the division on either flank, thereby forming a grid. Tactical circuits were then connected to strategic telegraph circuits.

In the late nineteenth century, as telephones became more common in civilian life, staff officers began to demand them to complement the telegraph. The Japanese made wide use of telephony during the Russo-Japanese war of 1904-05. Telephony also became very popular with staff officers during World War I so, in addition to line testing centres, many telephone switching centres appeared on the battlefield.

Radio

At the beginning of the 20th century, line communications were complemented by the new technology of wireless communication. Marconi had developed his first mobile wireless set in 1901 and the first British Army wireless telegraphy set was introduced in 1905. However, it was not until 1915 that a reasonably reliable set (the BF set) was introduced. Although the BF set was replaced by the more mobile loop-wireless set, both were still inefficient spark sets. The introduction in 1917 of the vacuum tube allowed for the production of CW sets that had, for the same power, greater selectivity, smaller antennas, and longer ranges.

Radio telegraphy was not readily accepted during World War I, as Marconi had only just achieved practical results. However, even early radio communications proved much more flexible than cable and it was not long before previously difficult tasks such as gun registration were being conducted by radio instead of line. Still, radio telegraphy was generally inefficient, mostly due to a poor understanding of the physical processes involved and the low frequencies used. Consequently, for the first few decades of the 20th Century, radio was looked upon by communicators as a supplementary means of communication, with line being the primary means.

Between the Wars

The period between the wars saw a number of developments in communications technology. The vacuum tube was perfected to provide the consistent amplification required for amplitude modulation and the first voice radio sets. The teletypewriter, or the printer telegraph, was developed, as was the field telephone set and the first small field switchboard.

During the 1930s, radio sets were developed to meet the necessary mobility, range and reliability required by the infantry, artillery, armour and aviation corps. In 1934, the US developed the first 'walkie talkie', which was used until replaced in 1943 by radios using the newly developed FM technique. These new crystal-controlled radios provided noise-free communications without the requirement to dial-tune, allowing the user to communicate at the push of a button.

World War II

During World War II, radio was used extensively at the tactical level for the first time. By the end of the war, all essential tactical and administrative communications was conducted by radio, mainly due to the inability of line to keep up with highly mobile, widely dispersed forces often operating in inhospitable terrain. However, line communications continued to be used during World War II, mostly for telephony. Large amounts of line were laid, particularly in those areas where radio communication were poor.

Although there were very few major advances in communications technology during World War II, by the end of the war military communications doctrine had changed considerably. Whilst line was still an important medium, the mobility and dispersion of the battlefield had reversed World War I doctrine so that radio was the primary means of communication and line was generally only used as a secondary means when time allowed it to be laid.

Two distinct battlefield communications needs had developed. The first type required high-capacity links to connect formation headquarters with units by line, radio or the signal dispatch service (SDS). Together, these infrastructure links became known as *trunk communications* in line with the terminology used for their civilian equivalents.

The second type of communications developed to allow units at brigade and below to perform tactical tasks. These links had to be flexible and responsive and under the direct control of the commander. Links were established using half-duplex, single-frequency, all-informed radio nets allowing the commander maximum flexibility to command a number of sub-units. These types of communications became known as *combat net radio*.

Doctrinally these divisions still exist on the modern battlefield, albeit in more sophisticated forms:

- **Combat Radio Sub-system.** The Combat Radio Sub-system comprises radio equipments operating in the HF, VHF and UHF bands and is the principal means of transmitting information among combat troops.

- **Trunk Communications Sub-system.** This Sub-system is the principal means of communication down to formation/unit and logistic installation level. The Sub-system comprises multi-channel radio equipment, line, switches and terminating facilities to provide voice, telegraph, facsimile, video and data communications as well as hand carriage.

CHARACTERISTICS OF MILITARY RADIO COMMUNICATIONS

Frequency Ranges

Before discussing the battlefield communications system, it is useful to examine that portion of the electromagnetic spectrum utilised by the Combat Radio and Trunk Communications Sub-systems. Frequency (wavelength) has a number of fundamental implications for military communications systems.

Capacity. Higher capacity (more or wider channels) requires more bandwidth. The number of channels available in each band increases roughly by a factor of ten, so the higher the frequency band; the more channels are available.

Quality. Better quality requires a more faithful reproduction of the baseband frequencies. This in turn requires a greater spread of modulated frequencies, and therefore a greater bandwidth to be transmitted. Therefore, in general, higher quality is available at higher frequencies.

Range. The lower the frequency, the longer the wavelength; the longer the wavelength, the less significant (relatively) become obstacles. In ground-wave communications, lower frequencies mean longer ranges (or conversely higher frequencies, shorter ranges) since free-space loss is inversely proportional to the square of frequency. In general, due to the dispersion of the modern battlefield, longer ranges are more desirable implying the need for lower frequencies.

Antenna Size. Antenna length is directly related to wavelength - an efficient antenna is either one or one-half wavelength long. Therefore, the higher the frequency, the smaller the antenna. Thus, higher frequencies allow the use of more manageable and more tactically deployable antennas. This must be balanced, however, with the greater pointing accuracy required for higher frequencies and less tolerance to obstacles in the path.

HF. HF frequencies are used for sky-wave or surface-wave working.

- **Surface Wave.** Due to the long wavelengths utilised, HF surface-wave propagation is generally reliable and has a reasonably good range. Even in poor soil conditions, ranges of 30 to 50 km are possible.

- **Sky Wave.** At skywave frequencies, ranges of thousands of kilometres are possible with relatively low powers. Skywave communications currently provide one of the few options available to communicate over the large distances required for widely dispersed deployments.

- **Dead Zone.** One of the difficulties with HF working is the gap between the longest surface-wave range and the shortest sky-wave range available with in-service antennas and available frequencies. Unfortunately, the ranges required by deployment in areas such as the former Republic of Yugoslavia will produce a significant number of dead zones, which can only be alleviated by the employment of specialised near-vertical incidence antennas.

VHF. At VHF the effects of screening by terrain, buildings, and trees become more significant. In addition to free-space loss, large differences in signal strength are possible within a small area due to reflection and diffraction loss. The greater bandwidth available allows the use of FM, which provides much better noise immunity.

UHF. At UHF frequencies, screening is very significant and propagation is generally limited to line-of-sight. Like VHF, there can be large differences in received signal strengths over a small area. UHF frequencies are of little use to combat radio due to the very short ranges available, although some use is found in short-range applications, particularly for use in section radios. However, the high bandwidths available mean that UHF is very desirable for trunk communications.

Analogue Modulation

The next major characteristic of communication is the method of modulation, which normally is AM (SSB) for HF, and FM for VHF and UHF.

AM. SSB transmission is normally used at HF since it allows close spacing of channels with a transmission bandwidth equal to the original message bandwidth.

FM. FM occupies a wider bandwidth than AM but the transmission is much more immune than AM to the effect of noise. The capture effect also suppresses weak signals. FM radios therefore tend not to have any of the background noise experienced on AM equipments. FM provides better quality but the need for a wide bandwidth (about eight times that required for SSB) means that it is employed only at VHF and higher frequencies.

So which frequency range and modulation type should we be using for combat radio and trunk communication? What factors should affect our decision? It is obvious from the above discussion that the decision to use one frequency rather than the other depends on the value judgement of whether range is more important than quality and capacity. This is discussed in the following section.

COMBAT RADIO

Combat radio is the primary means of communications to support tactical operations at brigade level and below. It provides simple, flexible, mobile, all-informed communications under the direct control of the commander. Armies generally employ two forms of combat radio:

- **Combat Net Radio (CNR),** which is used by combat troops is stringently designed for working in the harsh environment of the battlefield and in a hostile and congested electromagnetic environment.

- **Commercial Radio (CR),** which makes use of radios designed for robust civilian usage and is therefore well suited to internal security and other military use in areas, such as logistic areas, where the full cost of military ruggedisation cannot be justified.

CNR

CNR radio sets are generally grouped into nets to support tactical operations. One radio (normally that of the commander) is designated the *net control station (NCS)*. CNR nets are *all-informed, single-frequency, half-duplex* nets.

- **All-informed.** CNR nets are all-informed so that all stations can receive transmissions from any other station. For combat troops this is essential so that commanders can pass orders efficiently to a number of sub-units without having to repeat calls. Additionally, overall net traffic is reduced since all stations can remain informed of the general state of the unit and the battlefield by monitoring the net.

- **Single-frequency, half-duplex.** For simplicity (and therefore reduced size and weight), CNR radios transmit and receive on the same frequency. Users can therefore speak and listen, but not at the same time. That is, the radio operates in the half-duplex mode. Net discipline must therefore be im-posed on the users through the implementation of a protocol - *voice procedure*.

The decision to use a particular frequency depends on the desired compromise between range and quality and capacity. Whilst HF can provide long range communications, the quality and capacity are poor. Despite this, there are many military circumstances when long ranges are essential. For closer communications, combat troops prefer VHF frequencies, which provide the best compromise between range and quality/capacity. There is sufficient range (20km to 40km depending on terrain) and sufficient bandwidth available to use FM, which dramatically improves quality. Whilst large capacity (high quality) is available at UHF, range is limited to line-of sight. Table 6.1 summarises these considerations for application of each RF bands to battlefield communications.

CNR Improvements

Early use of radio on the battlefield provided an alternative to line as part of trunk communications. Soon, however, radio was used to connect observation posts to artillery batteries and so on. This avoided the laying of hundreds of miles of cable to support major offensives. Radio sets (and particularly their antenna systems) were initially too large to be of any great use to infantry. However, as sets and antennas reduced in size, they began to be employed to form artillery-infantry nets and infantry-armour nets.

By the end of WWII, the US had deployed FM CNR to most elements of the combat arms. Since then, there have been a number of advances in technology:

- sets have become lighter, smaller and more reliable due to smaller integrated circuit components requiring less space, power and maintenance;
- frequency synthesisers;
- ATUs have become smaller and integrated into the set;
- crypto has become smaller, integrated into the set or handset, uses over-the-air-rekeying (OTAR) etc;
- batteries have become smaller and allow longer transmit/receive times;
- better modems are available; and
- small improvements have been made in antenna design.

Band	Net Application	Advantages	Disadvantages
HF	• Company / battalion / brigade nets • rear links • armoured / reconnaissance / engineer / administration nets • special forces patrols	• cheap, man-portable, long range communications • graceful degradation of grade of service from data through voice to low-speed Morse	• short surface wave range for vehicle whips • relatively immobile for sky wave • limited number of frequencies / small bandwidth available
VHF	• platoon /company /battalion / brigade nets • armoured / reconnaissance / engineer / administration nets	• trade-off between bandwidth / power / weight / size • sufficient bandwidth available for secure transmissions • reliable / robust	• half duplex unsuited to data • heavy, particularly for secure radio • limited to radio horizon (re-transmission required for >30km)
UHF	• platoon nets • artillery between guns • within administrative areas • ground-to-air • special forces patrols	• lightweight • hand-held • short-range • limited range provides a measure of security from intercept	• line-of-sight limits range • interface to VHF CNR means difficulty in passing data through platoon net to company

Table 6.1. Application of RF bands to combat radio.

However, these changes have been evolutionary rather than revolutionary and the tactical use of CNR has remained largely unchanged since WWII. The major difference is in the ability to pass data, although most CNR are still analogue radios and are not well placed to cope with the expansion in the volume of data expected in the next few years. Major improvements to the US SINCGARS radio have led to a significant increase in the ability to provide a tactical data internet. The UK BOWMAN project will take one step further and will introduce a digital, internetted radio.

Although wider availability of trunk communications will decrease the requirement of CNR at certain levels, CNR will continue to be the primary means of exercising command below brigade. Combat forces will still require all-informed voice communication. However, the need to pass data over CNR is increasing. In particular, the tempo and intensity of the modern battlefield requires versatile, reliable communications with greater capacity.

Current and planned command, weapons and real-time sensor systems have made it essential for the battlefield communications system to be able to pass large volumes of information over longer distances at all levels of command, and across existing unit and formation boundaries. It is no longer possible for the CNR and Trunk Communications Sub-systems to be considered to be separate systems. Information must be able to pass seamlessly from the lowest unit level to the highest headquarters level without being re-entered. This means that, rather than having interfaces between the two sub-systems, they must be integrated seamlessly. This leads to the requirement for an internetted, digital, CNR Sub-system as we will discuss shortly.

The electromagnetic environment is currently severely congested with worse to come. Future CNR will be required to operate using smaller bandwidths through bandwidth-efficient digital modulation techniques or spectrum-efficient techniques such as direct sequence spread spectrum.

Voice versus Data

One of the important issues in future CNR is the issue of voice versus data. Clearly, commanders like the all-informed nature of CNR that utilises voice communications. Yet, the modern battlefield requires the ability for the CNR Sub-system to pass large volumes of data and to be integrated seamlessly into the trunk network. The debate can be summarised as follows.

Advantages of Voice. The main advantage of voice is that it is the most familiar form of communication for commanders. It is also the natural form of communications for humans and one of the prime vehicles for commanders to exercise leadership. Voice:

• carries the personality of the speaker,
• allows users to exchange information in the most natural format, and
• can often provide the fastest means in urgent situations.

Advantages of Data. The main disadvantage of voice is that it conveys transient information, which must be written down or typed in to a database, if it is to be retained. The main advantage of data is that the information is in a form that can be quickly stored and supports the principle of 'single-point-of-entry'. In short, in addition to the advantages we discussed in Chapter 2, data has the advantages that accrue from the information being in digital form.

- Much of the routine information flowing on the battlefield lends itself to formatting (LOCSTATS, SITREPS, etc) and is well suited to transmission as data.
- Terminals do not need to be manned for information to flow.
- Messages can be acknowledged automatically.
- Messages can be prepared off-line, reducing transmission time and therefore reducing vulnerability to intercept.
- Messages can be pre-formatted to reduced transmission time and to assist in database entry.
- Error detection and correction techniques can be used to increase the probability that a message is received correctly.
- Data only needs to be entered once, allowing for seamless integration across tactical and network boundaries.
- Digital communications have improved resistance in a congested and hostile spectrum.

In summary, the prime means available to the commander to influence the contact battle is through the force of his personality. However, we know that a large quantity of battlefield information is well suited to the more efficient transmission of data. Whilst the transmission of information as data offers many advantages, the requirement will continue for a voice capability on combat radio, sufficient to allow emotion and personality to remain recognisable. Therefore the CNR Sub-system must carry both voice and data.

Future Developments

Future developments in CNR therefore fall into two main categories: further evolutionary development and revolutionary new capabilities. First, modern technology will continue to extend current capabilities to provide radios that are:

- more microprocessor controlled;
- smaller and more robust;
- fully secure to all levels;
- inter-operable with in-service trunk networks and with the CNR and trunk networks of other services and allies;
- operated with automatic power control and frequency selection;
- robust and survivable in conventional and NBC environments; and
- flexible, reliable, simple to operate, and easy to manage and maintain.

However, future CNR will also require revolutionary new capabilities to:

- provide flexible communications modes with sufficient capacity to cope with high volumes of data without affecting the commander's ability to use voice;
- seamlessly integrate the CNR and Trunk Sub-systems so that all forms of communication (particularly data, voice and video) can be passed from one to another without operator involvement, which implies that CNR is:
  - digital; and
  - able to be internetted so that messages are automatically relayed from one radio to another.
- operate in a hostile electromagnetic environment and incorporate a range of Electronic Protection (EP) measures, which might include:
  - frequency hopping;
  - direct sequence spread spectrum;
  - free-channel search;
  - steerable null antennas;
  - automatic power control; and
  - anti-spoofing.

Commercial Radio

Commercial radio can be used in any location that is not subjected to all the rigorous battlefield conditions for which CNR is designed. Internal security operations and the guarding of large areas such as airfields or storage depots are examples of such situations. The radios can be small and will work on small power supplies if a central booster station (a *talkthrough*) is employed with a well-sited antenna. The use of relatively cheap commercial sets, instead of military sets, results in a considerable capital saving.

Commercial systems such as cellular radio systems are also finding application on the battlefield to provide access to the trunk network. These systems provide a viable alternative to the mobile access systems described in the next section.

Commercial radio has the advantages of being cheap compared to CNR, easy to operate, smaller and lighter than CNR, and able be introduced into service quickly. Disadvantages include a lack of robustness, and a lack of interoperability between different systems.

In-service commercial radio systems are normally designed to operate on one of a number of pre-set frequencies or channels. An all-informed net is normally provided by using the *two-frequency, half-duplex* system of operation.

TRUNK COMMUNICATIONS

Trunk communications provide headquarters with a backbone of high-capacity circuits required to pass large quantities information between commanders and staffs. Within the Trunk Communications Sub-system there are three major means by which information is passed: *radio*, including satellite; *line*, including fibre optics; and *hand carriage* (signal dispatch service).

Trunk radio and line circuits must be able to pass, in an efficient manner, voice, data, facsimile, telegraph and video. The ability of commanders and staff officers to speak to each other is fundamental to the successful negotiation of the C2 Cycle. The passage of facsimile and telegraph messages is equally essential to exchange documents and text. As more computers are present on the battlefield, facsimile and telegraph are being replaced by data, which must be transferred at ever increasing speeds. Despite rapid advances in technology, there are still many communications that are too bulky and are best transferred between headquarters by the Signal Dispatch Service (SDS).

Network Topologies

Within a headquarters, commanders and staff officers are connected by local telephone lines to a computer-controlled telephone exchange which provides subscribers with connections to other subscribers within the headquarters and with access to other headquarters via inter-exchange, or common-user trunk, circuits. Over the years, these trunk networks have developed from rudimentary chain-of-command networks providing voice and telegraph, to modern area trunk systems providing the full range of subscriber facilities.

First-generation Networks

As illustrated in Figure 6.1, communications in early trunk networks followed the chain of command requiring headquarters to act as both tactical bases and large communications nodes.

This dual role caused serious conflict between the communications requirement to have access to sufficiently high terrain, and the desire of the headquarters to conceal its location. The inclusion of the communications elements with the headquarters also seriously hampered mobility and any movement of the headquarters or damage to the network caused a disproportionate disruption to communications. Finally, because analogue transmission techniques were used, secure speech was impractical and only telegraph signals could be encrypted.

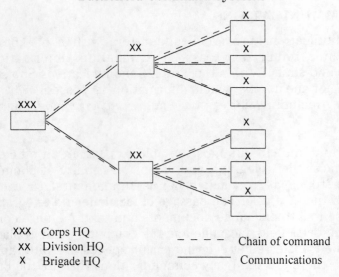

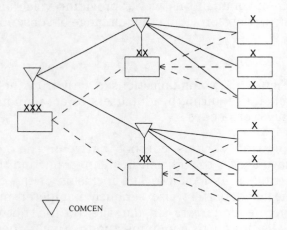

Figure 6.1. Direct chain-of-command trunk network.

Second-generation Networks

Figure 6.2 shows a second-generation trunk network, in which the tactical and communication roles of the headquarters were separated by creating a physically separate communications centre (COMCEN) which communicated to the headquarters over short cable links.

Figure 6.2. Displaced chain-of-command trunk network.

Tactical headquarters and communications sites could then be planned with a higher degree of independence (although the headquarters was still constrained by having to be near its COMCEN). The advent of data transmission also permitted encryption of each link to provide a secure speech network. An example of this type of network was the BRUIN network deployed by the British Army in north-west Europe from the 1960s until 1985 when it was replaced by PTARMIGAN.

Third-generation Networks

The next logical step was to remove the fixed relationship between the headquarters and its COMCEN, allowing a headquarters to deploy as required and the communications planners to provide one or more COMCENs that were able to serve the complex. Figure 6.3 illustrates an example of this third-generation, *expanded chain-of-command network*.

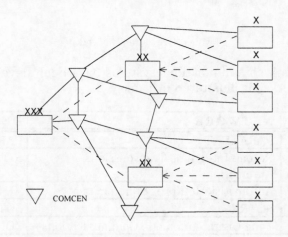

Figure 6.3. Expanded chain-of-command trunk network.

This configuration has the additional advantage of being able to provide duplication (redundancy) so that headquarters could move without disrupting the network. The network could also be reconfigured manually without disrupting communications, thereby improving network reliability. An example of a third-generation network is the US Army's Army Tactical Communications System (ATACS), which was deployed until the mid-1990s when it was finally replaced by the Mobile Subscriber Equipment (MSE) trunk system.

Fourth-generation Networks

The logical extension of these developments is the fourth generation, *area trunk network* illustrated in Figure 6.4.

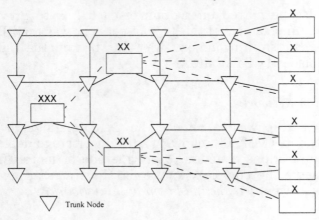

Figure 6.4. Area trunk network.

Most modern trunk communications systems have been developed as fourth-generation networks, as illustrated in Table 6.2.

COUNTRY	NETWORK	DESIGNATION
Australia	PARAKEET	PARAKEET
France / Belgium	Réseau Intégré de Transmissions Automatique	RITA
Germany	Automatisierte Korps-Stammnetz	AUTOKO
Italy	SOTRIN	SOTRIN
The Netherlands	Zone Digital Automatic Communications	ZODIAC
United Kingdom	PTARMIGAN	PTARMIGAN
United States	Mobile Subscriber Equipment	MSE

Table 6.2. National trunk networks.

An area trunk network provides a grid of switching centres (or nodes) laid out to give area coverage. Nodes are interconnected by multi-channel radio relay bearers, which are normally point-to-point UHF or SHF radio links. Increasingly, however, links between nodes are provided by satellite communications to provide coverage of larger areas. Within the network, headquarters can move about as required to meet the demands of the tactical situation, connecting by radio relay to the nearest node. Access is provided for individual mobile subscribers and CNR users.

An area network contains significant redundancy and can sustain considerable damage because of the alternative routes available. Nodes have much more freedom, allowing rapid movement to reconfigure as required by the tactical situation or network outages. The obvious disadvantage of an area network is the significant amount of equipment and manpower required to establish the large number of nodes. This disadvantage is by far outweighed, however, by greatly improved flexibility, reliability, survivability and capacity.

The flexibility of modern area networks is dramatically illustrated when operational circumstances dictate deployments outside the context of the Cold War environment in north-west Europe, for which they were designed. In the Gulf War, both PTARMIGAN and MSE were often employed as linear communications systems to keep up with the rapid rate of advance of the land battle. In the Gulf, and in more recent operations in Europe, the large scale of deployments and the wide separation of small pockets of troops has forced communications planners to provide smaller 'islands' (called *enclaves*) of area network interconnected by satellite communications. Since the end of the Cold War, this architecture now appears likely to be the norm, rather than an exception.

Network Components

Whilst each nation tends to differ in its implementation of a trunk network, most employ area networks that have many common components. The basic building blocks of the trunk network are the *trunk nodes*, which are connected together by *radio relay* to provide an infrastructure of multi-channel trunk links. Headquarters and command posts connect to the network, and thence to each other, through *access nodes*. Mobile network subscribers are catered for through *Single Channel Radio Access (SCRA)* and combat forces can interface through a *CNR Interface (CNRI)*. Interfaces to other trunk networks are provided by a *Tactical Interface Installation (TII)*. The following sections provide more detail on each of these components, which are discussed in generic terms.

Trunk Nodes

Trunk nodes are deployed to provide a generic deployment of an area network covering the area of operations. Typically, there are approximately forty trunk nodes in a corps network. Each division will control approximately four and the remainder will be deployed as corps assets. Each node is identical in architecture, but will deploy in varying configurations depending on the tactical situation. The network is deployed with a logical grid connectivity but will have varying physical configurations since the location of the trunk nodes is dictated by the terrain and the tactical situation.

Nodes are deployed and re-deployed to allow the network to change shape to adjust to the needs of combat forces as the tactical battle requires. Nodes can be withdrawn from the network and re-deployed to facilitate an advance, withdrawal, or movement to a flank. Network density can also be modified to cope with changes in force composition and deployment. Figure 6.5 illustrates the basic components of a trunk node.

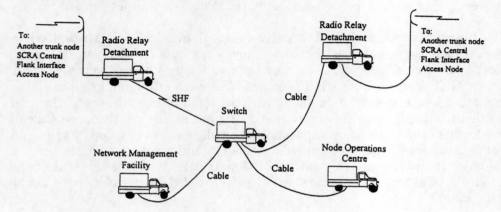

Figure 6.5. The basic components of a typical trunk node site.

Switch. The heart of each node is the processor-controlled digital switch, which is an automatic circuit switch that invariably incorporates a packet switch. The switch typically has at least 16 or 32 trunk channels for inter-nodal trunking. One channel is generally allocated to engineering and the remainder are encrypted and assigned to interconnection with other nodal switches, access nodes, and SCRA. Each node switch is normally connected through radio relay to three other node switches to ensure a robust, survivable network.

Node Operations Centre (NOC). The NOC contains an operator interface to assist in engineering the switch, trunk encryption equipment and some limited patching. The NOC could be a separate vehicle or located in the switch vehicle.

Node Management Facility (NMF). The NMF performs link management for the radio relay links connected to the switch including link engineering and frequency management. Normally some functions are also performed on behalf of the System Control Centre (SCC), the next level of management in the network. Normally the NMF is a separate vehicle, manned by the trunk node commander.

Radio Relay Detachments. Typically, four or five radio relay detachments are deployed in each trunk node. Each detachment can terminate radio links from approximately three other radio relay detachments. Detachments are normally sited on a suitable terrain feature and are connected to the node switch by a cable 'tail' or by SHF 'down-the-hill' radio.

Radio Relay

The multi-channel, digital links between trunk nodes could be provided by any wide-band communications medium. Although it is possible to lay line with sufficient bandwidth for trunk traffic, radio systems are far more flexible and are normally the preferred method of linking trunk nodes.

Multi-Channel. Modern networks currently provide at least 16 or 32 times 16kbps time division multiplexed channels on inter-nodal links. Of these channels, one is allocated to engineering and network management, two are used to interface local switchboards, three or four are permanently allocated to the packet switch network and the remainder are available for trunk links between subscribers. Most networks now plan to provide trunk links of up to 2Mbps.

Frequency. The UHF and SHF bands are normally utilised to provide the bandwidth required by radio relay links. The frequency of operation of trunk radio links is selected as a trade-off between the need for high capacity (higher frequency) and ease of antenna alignment (lower frequency). At the high end, SHF systems are constrained by line-of-sight, requiring careful selection of sites, high masts and highly directional antennas that take a long time to erect and align. Therefore, SHF systems normally cannot meet tactical mobility constraints that demand a short time into and out of action. Instead, UHF is favoured as a reasonable military compromise between adequate channel capacity and tactical mobility. Three UHF bands are commonly utilised: Band I - 225-400MHz; Band II - 610-960MHz; and Band III - 1350-1850MHz.

Antennas. As radio relay links are point-to-point, directional antennas are used to maximize gain in one direction and make the best use of available power. Directional antennas also reduce the radiation in unwanted directions, which reduces interference on neighbouring radio systems and minimizes the possibility of interception and jamming. Antenna gain is limited to about 10-25dB so that alignment and concealment are straightforward.

Siting. Since the two sites may be some distance apart, the radio relay site is normally connected to the asset it is serving by a cable or, for longer distances, an SHF down-the-hill radio link.

Radio Relay Relay. Often two trunk nodes cannot be connected by one link and *radio relay relay* is required. The relay station is sited so that signals received from each terminal can be automatically re-transmitted to the other. Where long inter-nodal links are required to support widely dispersed forces, there may be several relay stations. Often, however, satellite links are preferred.

Satellite Network Links

Area trunk communications networks were designed to provide reliable, survivable communications within a corps area. With the demise of the Cold War, such deployments are less common. In fact, the largest use of trunk networks in recent conflicts has been in the Gulf War, where despite supporting corps deployments, trunk networks had great difficulty in keeping up with the rapid rate of advance and still providing an area architecture. Consequently, networks were invariably deployed in a linear fashion, requiring some quick re-engineering of software to cope with the increased distances between switches. The main difficulty was in the inability of radio relay detachments to provide the necessary nodal inter-connections over the large distances required to support the advance.

A similar problem has arisen, for slightly different reasons, in major deployments since the Gulf War. In the various national deployments in the former Republic of Yugoslavia it has been impossible to provide a terrestrial area network due to the nature of the employment, particularly the inability to secure terrain between dispersed units and formations. Radio relay relay is therefore very difficult to deploy, due to the long range of the inter-nodal links and the difficulty in finding secure sites for relays.

The solution to both of these problems has been the introduction of satellite trunk links to extend the range of inter-nodal connections to cross inhospitable, or unsecured terrain. As illustrated in Figure 6.6, this does not affect the logical layout of the area network, but dramatically increases the range of inter-nodal links. Area networks are still provided locally and satellite links are provided to link these network 'enclaves' together.

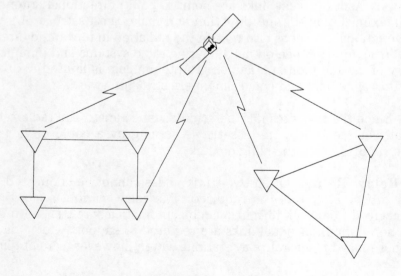

Figure 6.6. Area network employing satellite internodal links.

In addition to satellite links, connections between nodes can also be extended by troposcatter communications, or connections through commercial communications networks. However, troposcatter terminals are much larger than satellite terminals and such systems generally have lower bandwidths. Commercial systems are not always available or survivable enough for inclusion in trunk networks. Satellite trunk links are therefore usually preferred to span large distances between nodes.

Access Nodes

Subscribers gain access to the trunk network through an *access node*, which is a processor-controlled digital switch capable of handling the number of subscribers at the access point. At least two levels of access node are normally provided: small access node for brigade headquarters and a large access node for divisional headquarters and above. Some networks provide access nodes to lower levels - at regimental or battalion command posts. In most networks, however, access to these levels is provided through SCRA, which is described in the following section.

Access nodes are connected to the network through radio relay. Large access nodes are normally always connected to two trunk nodes; small access nodes are normally only connected to one, with a standby link engineered in case of failure. Small access nodes normally provide for approximately 25 subscribers and the large access nodes provide for approximately 150 subscribers. Both types of nodes have the facilities to interconnect to satellite or troposcatter links, or to commercial carriers. Figure 6.7 shows a simplified layout of a small access node.

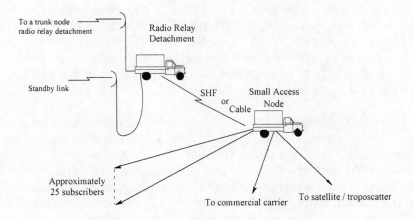

Figure 6.7. A small access node.

As illustrated in Figure 6.8, the large access node has a similar layout, albeit with more subscribers. The large access node also contains a node operations centre (NOC) and a network management facility (NMF), similar to those found in the node centre of a trunk node.

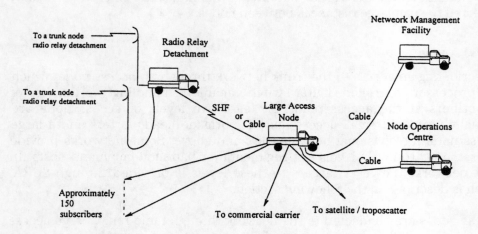

Figure 6.8. A large access node.

SCRA

Access for mobile or isolated subscribers is provided through SCRA, which provides duplex VHF radio access to the trunk network. SCRA provides individual mobile users with network facilities (voice, data, telegraph and facsimile) equivalent to those available to static subscribers of an access node. The SCRA Sub-system consists of two major elements - *subscriber terminals* and *radio access points (RAP)* through which subscribers access the trunk network. RAPs are normally connected to one trunk node, with a standby link engineered to another. Connection to trunk nodes can be via cable, SHF down-the-hill radio, or UHF radio relay link.

RAP. Each RAP can accept approximately 50 mobile subscribers affiliated within a 15km radius. However, an RAP can normally only cope with simultaneous calls from a smaller number of subscribers (approximately 10). The actual range between the RAP and subscriber will depend on the terrain, antenna heights and weather conditions. For example, a mobile subscriber can generally double the range by stopping and erecting an elevated antenna. Figure 6.9 shows a simplified layout of an RAP site, which consists of an RAP vehicle containing transmitters and receivers connected to one or more omnidirectional antennas. RAPs are deployed to provide overlapping areas of coverage, which provide continuous coverage for a mobile user who can move between areas. RAPs are normally able to operate on two or three power settings so that, on call initiation with each mobile subscriber, an appropriate power level can be chosen to reduce the RF signature of the RAP.

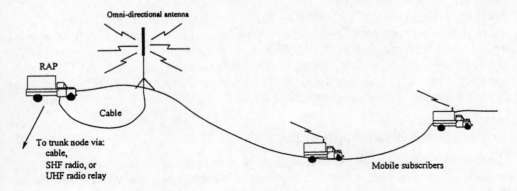

Figure 6.9. Simplified layout of an RAP.

Subscriber Terminals. A mobile subscriber is given a unique identification number during a process called *affiliation*, through which the subscriber is recognised and his identity is validated. The affiliation process differs between networks but normally entails a deliberate action on the part of the subscriber to affiliate for the first time. In some networks, such as PTARMIGAN, the subscriber must affiliate each time connection to a new RAP is required. If the RAP number is not known, a search can be initiated to find the most suitable RAP. In other networks such as MSE, re-affiliation is automatic as the subscriber is handed over from one RAP to another whilst driving through the network. Upon affiliation, the power output of the terminal is normally reduced to the minimum possible power level to reduce adjacent channel interference from a strong signal on a frequency adjacent to that from a terminal further away. Automatic power control is essential at the terminal end of the link to ensure similar power levels at the RAP from all subscribers.

Direct Access. In some networks, such as Germany's AUTOKO and The Netherland's ZODIAC, mobile subscribers in close proximity within the same RAP area can contact each other directly. This reduces traffic load on the RAP, which is only used to relay the call if the direct connection cannot be made within a specified time.

CNRI

SCRA provides network access to mobile network subscribers, generally giving the same facilities as subscribers in command posts. Most networks provide an additional form of access to troops who are not network subscribers but who can use their CNR to make temporary, limited access to the network. The CNRI provides a semi-automatic interface between a CNR user and the network. Each CNRI vehicle allows two or three VHF and two or three HF CNR users to make semi-automatic access to the network. In each frequency band, the CNRI vehicle has a hailing radio through which CNR users make contact with the operator. The operator sets up the call, which is established through one of the VHF or HF traffic radios. Calls made from the network are automatic and do not require operator intervention. As CNR nets are single-frequency, half-duplex, CNRI only provides rudimentary access to network facilities. The range of CNRI depends on the CNR frequency band.

Tactical Interface Installation (TII)

Most modern networks provide direct access to trunk networks from other nations. This was particularly important in Western Europe when each corps had to provide communication to flanking formations from other nations. Within NATO, inter-network interface for analogue signals, voice and telegraph, is arranged through use of the STANAG 5040 standard. Interoperability between digital EUROCOM systems using 16kbps modulation is provided by STANAG 4200. The vehicle allocated to such an interface is called the *Tactical Interface Installation (TII)*. In the future, NATO partners will attempt to remove the need for gateways to interconnect trunk networks and battlefield command systems through the use of common standards that should allow such systems to interoperate directly.

Trunk Subscriber Facilities

Trunk networks provide static and mobile subscribers with secure voice, data, telegraph and facsimile services. The following paragraphs describe the equipment and facilities provided to subscribers.

Subscriber Equipment. Subscribers have a digital or analogue telephone through which voice calls can be made through the digital circuit-switched network. A *data adapter* provides data, facsimile and telegraph facilities. Analogue-to-digital conversion (normally some form of delta modulation) is performed in the equipment to provide an output data rate, normally at 16kbps.

Security. Encryption for the trunk network is provided through bulk encryption of the trunk links. The network is therefore normally treated as a SECRET-high. That is, all recipients of voice or data are assumed to be appropriately cleared, or that there are physical security measures in place to ensure that only appropriately cleared personnel can receive the information. Should this not be possible, or higher classifications are desired, links between users can be individually encrypted once a circuit has been established. This form of double encryption is commonly used for intelligence and electronic warfare circuits.

Voice Services. Since subscribers can move about within the network, most modern networks give each subscriber a unique number called a *directory number*. Most networks use the NATO 7-digit deducible directory (STANAG 5046), in which the subscriber's directory number is deducible from his unit and appointment. Normal PABX voice facilities such as call hold, transfer and call forward are provided along with compressed dialling, abbreviated dialling and conference facilities. Particular military requirements are met by the *precedence* and *pre-emption* facilities. Pre-emption allows selected subscribers with a higher precedence to manually over-ride other callers if the called extension is busy. A subscriber can be located at any time through *affiliation* and *flood search*.

- **Affiliation.** Each subscriber is required to affiliate to the network through the switch to which he or she is currently connected. The switch holds a record of the subscriber's identity and precedence and the facilities available to that particular user. Through affiliation, each user tells the network where (on which telephone) he or she is currently located.

- **Flood Search.** Subscribers are located by the network through a flood-search mechanism where the switch to which the calling subscriber is connected calls all other switches sequentially until the called subscriber's parent switch responds. Once the subscriber's location has been identified, the connection can be made.

Data Services. Data services are normally provided by a packet-switched network integrated into the circuit-switched network. Although voice and data are both transmitted as a digital stream in a digital trunk network, the two transmissions have different requirements. Voice circuits (digital or analogue) are best handled using circuit switching; data transmission is most efficiently handled using packet switching. Circuit and packet switching within the same trunk network are normally integrated by embedding the packet-switches in the circuit-switched network.

Characteristics of Modern Trunk Networks

Several basic characteristics distinguish the latest generation of military trunk systems from earlier generations.

Commonality. The concept of convergence requires that a single type of switch can route voice, data, facsimile, telegraph and video around the network. We saw earlier that voice and data require different switching techniques. Video has different requirements again and can only be handled in current systems by setting up a circuit-switched channel that is allocated for the duration of the video transfer. In future trunk networks, a single switch is required to efficiently handle voice, data, telegraph, facsimile and video. This is the great promise of asynchronous transfer mode (ATM), which will be fielded within the next decade in networks such as MSE. Then, bandwidth can be dynamically allocated and managed on a priority basis, and all forms of users can be accommodated efficiently.

Capacity. The provision of sufficient capacity has always been a significant problem in the deployment of a tactical communications system. However, the rapid growth in communications requirements has meant that systems must provide significantly large bandwidths than in the past. Currently, networks provide data rates of the order of 2Mbps on trunk links. Near-term improvements will see rates increase to between 4Mbps and 10Mbps, with mid-term requirements increasing beyond that. This requirement for higher capacities in trunk links has two significant problems:

• **Switching.** Network switches must be able to cope with these volumes of information. ATM promises to provide a solution to this problem through the ability to switch at high speeds.

• **Trunk Links.** Trunk links, particularly radio, must be able to cope with the significantly higher bandwidths. Terrestrial radio links will struggle to provide the desired capacities as higher frequencies will be required, reducing the planning ranges between radio relay detachments. The use of satellite communications will therefore increase since they offer sufficient bandwidths without the range limitations.

Upgrade Path. Most military communications equipment has at least a 10-year gestation period from conception to introduction into service. The technology implemented is at least five, and more often, ten years old when the equipment is fielded. The life of type of such equipment is approximately 20 years so that, at the end of its life, the technology employed by a radio system may be 30 years old. That was barely acceptable in the last few generations of equipment, but it is totally unacceptable in the next generation of equipments. Since bandwidth requirements are predicted to double every three or four years, a new approach to equipment procurement is required. Equipment must be specified, designed and procured in a modular fashion so that multiplexers, modems, amplifiers, etc can individually replaced to meet new requirements without having to dispose of the whole system. The equipment must be designed and fielded with the expectation that it will undergo at least four or five major modifications during its in-service life of 15 to 20 years. Fortunately such a philosophy has become more accepted in recent years and has begun to be incorporated in most national Defence procurement guidelines.

Network Management

As trunk networks have matured and have become less aligned with the chain of command, separate network management has had to evolve, and in many respects has become more complicated. The aim of network management is to provide and maintain effective and reliable communications, which implies the following management tasks:

- a communications appreciation
- development of a plan for network connectivity,
- allocation of resources,
- preparation and issue of orders,
- frequency assignment,
- network monitoring,
- traffic engineering,
- management of network outages and node movement,
- management of cryptographic equipment and codes,
- system maintenance,
- implementation of electronic protection measures,
- interface to CNR and other trunk networks, and
- system performance analysis.

Network managers must provide a well-balanced, well-engineered network that provides sufficient capacity and adequate coverage. This is a similar requirement to the management of civilian networks. However, the task becomes at least an order of magnitude more difficult when the network is frequently re-deploying to avoid detection and destruction and the user communities are continually moving and re-connecting. Network management is arguably the most important function in an area network. Sadly, it is one that is often overlooked until introduction into service, despite the fact that there are many tools to assist.

SDS

SDS is normally provided by signals units to hand-carry messages and information from one location to another on the battlefield. The main dispatch services which are used for SDS are: the dispatch rider service, mounted in vehicles or on motor cycles; and the aerial dispatch service, which may have aircraft on permanent allocation or make use other aircraft as they are available.

The main advantages of SDS compared with radio and line systems are security capacity, and freedom from transmission errors. The main disadvantages of SDS are that it is labour intensive, the service is slow compared with other means, and safe routes must be selected.

COMMUNICATIONS ELECTRONIC WARFARE

We saw in Chapter 1 that domination of the electromagnetic spectrum is critical. The C2 Cycle depends very heavily on the electromagnetic spectrum to maximise the effectiveness of STA, communications and information systems. If these systems are destroyed degraded or deceived, the C2 Cycle will not operate correctly and the commander and staff will not adequately be able to prosecute war. Such lessons are scattered throughout military history and future commanders neglect them at their peril. The capability to conduct electronic combat and dominate the electromagnetic spectrum is an essential component of any modern force structure.

EW is an area of considerable innovation. The introduction of new and more capable communications equipment will require more capable EW equipment, which will in turn drive the development of more sophisticated communications equipment. EW capabilities are highly classified to protect a vital edge in any future conflict and most parametric data are jealously guarded, However, EW techniques are generally unclassified and are covered briefly in the following sections.

For convenience, EW can be divided into *communications EW* and *non-communications EW* (comms & non-comms EW). Communications EW is principally targeted against CNR and trunk communications whilst non-communications EW is targeted against emitters such as radars. Here, we are concerned fundamentally with communications EW, the sub-divisions of which are *Electronic Support (ES)*, *Electronic Attack (EA)*, and *Electronic Protection (EP)*. ES, EA and EP were previously known respectively as Electronic Support Measures (ESM), Electronic Counter Measures (ECM), and Electronic Counter-Counter Measures (ECCM).

Electronic Support (ES)

ES is defined as:

That division of EW involving actions tasked by, or under direct control of, an operational commander to search for, intercept, identify and locate sources of intentional and unintentional radiated electromagnetic energy for the purposes of immediate threat recognition.

The ES process involves *search*, *intercept*, *monitoring*, *direction finding (DF)* and *analysis*. ES has three main functions, to produce battlefield intelligence, to provide steerage for EA, and to cue STA resources.

Search

Search involves the reconnaissance of the electronic activity in the electromagnetic spectrum to classify the transmissions occurring within it. Searching can be conducted in general terms, or it can be more specific to look for particular call signs, types of modulation or other signal or traffic characteristics.

The frequency range of interest can be searched by two main types of receivers: *scanning* and *channelised*. A scanning receiver is swept across the frequency band to identify active transmissions. The disadvantage of this approach is that, while it is acceptable for long-duration signals, it can only examine a narrow portion of the frequency spectrum at any one point in time. Short-duration signals, and particularly frequency hopping transmissions, may not be detected. Such signals are better found using a channelised receiver in which many narrow-band filters are employed in parallel to cover a complete band simultaneously. Although frequency resolution of channelised receivers can be lower than scanning receivers, it is generally good enough to ensure that a signal is detected so that it can be used to direct more-detailed search.

Intercept and Monitoring

Once intercepted, the emission can be classified by its external characteristics (frequency, bandwidth, power, etc) and by the information contained within. If desired, the transmission is monitored to extract the information, which can take a number of forms. Net activity can always be monitored, even if the net is encrypted and the internal content is not available. Monitoring of an un-encrypted net will reveal call signs, procedures and possible locations as well as a wealth of tactical information. The ES receiver settings can be transferred to DF receivers to obtain lines of bearing to the transmitter.

DF

DF can be used to determine the approximate location of emitters. It should be noted that at communications frequencies battlefield DF accuracies are in the order of $\pm 2°$ rms. At a range of 30 km, this leads to an uncertainty of 1km in the position of the emitter. Further refinement of the location of the emitter can be gained by an analysis of the map to determine likely locations within the DF error. Whilst DF accuracy is sufficient for intelligence purposes, it is not generally accurate enough for target acquisition.

DF uses the basic principle of triangulation where at least three DF receivers are positioned on a baseline to find the position of an emitter. Each DF receiver has a special antenna that is used to take a bearing towards the emitter. The bearings are plotted on a map, either manually or automatically, to form a triangle that should contain the emitter. The size of the triangle will depend on the accuracy of each bearing that depends on a number of variables: such as the site of the DF stations and radio path factors.

Analysis

Finally, analysis is carried out in an attempt to put together a comprehensive electronic order of battle. The signal characteristics, information content and location are analysed to provide an overall picture of the enemy's deployment. Conclusions are usually drawn about activity, future intentions, headquarter locations, unit types and formation boundaries. However, as with any intelligence, care must be taken to ensure that the conclusions are tested against collateral (other intelligence) sources, to counter possible enemy deception techniques.

Electronic Attack

EA is defined as:

That division of EW involving the use of electromagnetic or directed energy to attack personnel, facilities, or equipment with the intent of degrading, neutralising or destroying enemy combat capability.

The sub-divisions of EA are *jamming*, *deception* and *neutralisation*.

Jamming

The aim of communications jamming is to disrupt enemy nets. The jammer aims to deliver more power at the receivers in the net, than is delivered by the intended transmitter. This requires the jammer either to be closer than the intended transmitter (which is unlikely in most tactical situations) or to transmit on higher power settings. This makes the jammer vulnerable to enemy ES and weapon systems. Therefore, the jammer is normally very mobile and does not stay in the same position for very long after jamming. Jammers also tend to operate in pairs; one jamming while the other is moving so that continuous jamming can be achieved while avoiding detection. Jamming is also rarely used without ES support to assist in determining how effective jamming has been. Jamming must also be carefully planned and controlled to avoid affecting friendly communications and ES assets.

The main types of jamming and their characteristics are outlined in Table 6.3.

Type	Nature	Advantages/Disadvantages
Spot	Single frequency High power	Minimum fratricide Inefficient us of power
Comb	Multiple simultaneous frequencies Medium power on each frequency	Efficient use of available jammer power
Barrage	Wide band jamming Reduced power on each frequency	High fratricide Inefficient
Swept	Wide coverage Concentrated power on each frequency	High fratricide More efficient than barrage
Responsive	Single frequency Concentrated power - only when target frequency is active	Efficient use of power Look-through capability required during jamming to see if net is still active

Table 6.3. Types of Communications Jamming.

The decision to jam may not be as straightforward as it initially seems. First, the desired effect must be decided. If it is intended to deny the enemy access to communications, then jamming must be comprehensive and simultaneously attack all forms of CNR and trunk communications. If an encrypted link is to be jammed to force the net into communicating in clear (or to identify alternate frequencies), then care must be taken to ensure that the enemy operators think that they are suffering from poor propagation, rather than jamming. Similarly, an isolated receiver can be jammed to increase net activity, help identify the net control station and give more time to DF each station. Therefore, the decision to jam is normally retained at a high level.

EA is one attack option available to the commander, who must decide whether it is the most appropriate compared to other forms such as artillery. Often it is more beneficial to monitor the net to gather intelligence than it is to jam. EA in direct support of an attack may present a different proposition. However, even then, it may be better to monitor a command net and identify the moment that the enemy commander commits reserves, than it is to deny access to communications and to have the reserves committed by some other means that cannot be intercepted as readily. Jamming may announce to an enemy that his use of the spectrum has been compromised, prompting him to change frequencies and therefore have to be found again. Additionally, use of jamming may disclose future intentions of friendly forces, such as a precursor to an attack.

Like fire support, jamming must be timed to occur at the appropriate point in battle. The enemy must not be given advance warning and time to utilise alternate means. Whilst they have dramatic impact on the modern battle, jamming assets are scarce and must be used judiciously. A jammer radiating at full power is a very vulnerable asset, which should not be put at risk lightly.

Effect on Modulation. Jamming has different effects on various forms of modulation:

- **AM.** In AM, the information is impressed on the amplitude of the carrier. An AM jamming signal appears to the receiver as co-channel interference and the operator will hear both the intended transmitter and the jammer in proportion to their received powers. Since the intended transmitter is much closer, the jammer is normally unable to provide sufficient power to totally swamp it. However, the AM jammer normally attempts to disrupt communications causing the net to become more active and reveal more information to ES assets. If desired, noise, tones, music or pre-recorded traffic can be used to modulate the jammer's carrier.

- **FM.** Due to the capture effect is easier for the jammer to exceed the required threshold and 'capture' the FM receiver than it is for the AM jammer to swamp the AM receiver. This occurs from a straight power calculation. If the jammer uses the carrier only to jam, the receiver will be captured, but the operator will hear nothing since there is no modulation present. Again, if desired, noise, tones, music or pre-recorded traffic can be used to modulate the jammer's carrier.

- **Digital Modulation.** Digital radio links are more difficult to jam because the jamming signal is treated as noise. Due to the nature of the PSK modulation and the error correction and detection techniques used, digital transmissions can operate (albeit at lower information rates) in the presence of more noise than analogue FM signals. However, once the link error margin is exceeded, digital links will fail completely.

Unattended Jammers (UAJs). The difficulty in jamming is to put enough power onto the intended receiver. UAJs are low-powered, low-cost jammers that are placed very close to the receiver and can therefore jam more effectively. A stand-off jammer would rarely be closer than 10km to its intended target; a UAJ could be placed closer than 1km. This closeness dramatically reduces the free-space loss for the jammer and the UAJ transmitted power only has to be one ten-thousandth of the power of the stand-off jammer. UAJs can be deployed by special forces, withdrawing troops, or by rocket or artillery shell. A range of deployment options are available, including an electronic minefield through which an enemy would have to advance or withdraw suffering severe loss of communication, with subsequent confusion and delay.

Deception

The aim of deception is to mislead or confuse the enemy. Deception can be achieved by transmitting false or misleading information as part of a deception operation, or EW operators can attempt to enter enemy nets and imitate a station to mislead or gain information. Previously recorded, genuine net traffic can also be re-transmitted for similar aims. Deception must be planned at the highest possible level and executed through a thorough plan.

Neutralisation

This aspect of EA involves the neutralisation of electronic equipment through the ability to damage or destroy equipment or to dazzle the operator. Forms of attack include *electromagnetic pulse (EMP)*, or more commonly on the modern battlefield, *directed energy weapons (DEW)*. DEW technology is still in its infancy and faces a number of technological and ethical issues before it is introduced in large numbers. We do not have room here to discuss it any further, but DEW is an increasing threat that future commanders will surely face.

Electronic Protection

EP is defined as:

That division of EW involving actions taken to protect personnel, facilities, and equipment from any effects of friendly or enemy employment of EW that degrade, neutralise, or destroy friendly combat capability.

EP encompasses defensive EW techniques to protect friendly use of the electromagnetic spectrum. It is an important area that is conducted by all operators of electronic equipment to reduce the effectiveness of enemy offensive EW. EP techniques fall into three broad categories:

- **Technical.** Technical measures are designed into communications equipment to provide resistance to jamming, reduce probability of intercept, or both. Techniques to resist jamming include null-steering antennas; direct sequence spread spectrum; and frequency hopping. Low probability of intercept techniques include spread spectrum and frequency hopping, automatic power control, and burst transmission.

- **Functional.** Reducing the effect of enemy EW is not just about technical solutions. Many functional procedures can be implemented by operators. For example, appropriate power settings, good antenna siting to utilise terrain screening, short transmission times, and good radio procedure will all reduce the possibility of intercept as well as opportunities for DF.

• **Tactical.** Tactical measures are collective operating measures designed to reduce the effect of enemy EW on friendly nets. These include: good net discipline, encryption, and good net procedures. Encryption is a vital component here. Enemy intelligence gathering is significantly reduced if the information contained within transmissions can be protected by encryption. The only information then available is obtained from DF as well as some analysis of signal characteristics.

SUMMARY

This chapter has presented a brief overview of battlefield communications systems and electronic warfare systems. The next chapter discusses battlefield information systems.

7.
Battlefield Information Systems

In the last chapter we discussed on the communications required to support the C2 Cycle. This chapter concentrates on the *information systems* that underpin command systems. Now, information systems (or computers) exist in many locations on the battlefield and most have roles to play in the C2 Cycle. However, we will concentrate on those systems provided to support the *Information Processing* and *Decision Making* half of the Cycle as illustrated in Figure 7.1.

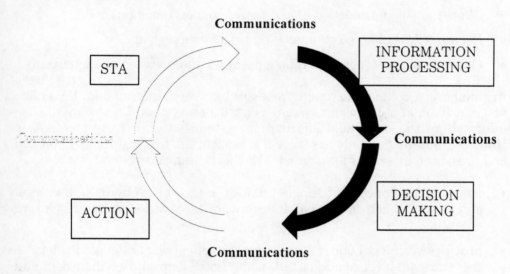

Figure 7.1. The right-hand half of the C2 Cycle.

Whilst we considered battlefield communications system in isolation in the last chapter, it must be recognised that battlefield information systems and their communications are inextricably linked. Few modern communications systems work without embedded computers and few computers work in isolation without connection to other computers. As illustrated in Figure 7.1, the information systems involved in the Information Processing and Decision Making half of the C2 Cycle rely heavily on communications. First, through interfaces to the tactical communications system, STA systems relay information to the headquarters and headquarters pass orders and information to combat forces. These are the communications depicted at the top and bottom of Figure 7.1. Second, the communications depicted on the right of Figure 7.1 are those between information systems involved in information processing and decision making. In fact, the communications that support those information systems can be considered to be depicted by the arrows on the right-hand side of the diagram.

COMMAND SYSTEMS

The automated component of the command system provides the commander and staff with support to the C2 process through the ability to complete the following:

- *Data Understanding* (data processing and synthesis into information);

- *Situation Analysis* (information analysis to infer environmental descriptions);

- *Planning* (the formulation of alternative courses of action);

- *Decision Making* (selection of appropriate courses); and

- *Communication* (between functional areas and between headquarters).

In summary, a command system processes battlefield information. If you like, you can think of a command system as a weapon system. The weapon is the information; the battlefield information system is the delivery mechanism. However, information only has value if it is accurate, timely, properly collated, and presented in a digestible format. The ideal command system:

- employs the concept of 'single point of entry', whereby data is entered and provided across tactical and network boundaries without being re-entered;

- provides seamless connectivity from the tactical (section/platoon) level to the strategic-level headquarters using battlefield and civilian communications systems;

- allows for horizontal and vertical integration;

- provides battlefield synchronisation;

- provides situational awareness - a common view of the battlefield in real time;

- allows commanders to concentrate combat power effectively and decisively;

- enables rapid fusion of data to become information, which is then available to all commanders;

- provides for rapid exchange of target data from sensor to weapons system and between weapon systems;

- allows commanders to command and control on the move; and

- is able to be used both within barracks and during tactical deployment.

Although information systems provide excellent support in rapidly processing large quantities of information, it is important to remember that they are simply a support tool and cannot currently reason or plan. They provide an excellent tool for the commander to help process the vast amount of information available; but they cannot currently replace reasoning and planning ability.

Domains

As illustrated in Figure 7.2(a), NATO, and thence ABCA, have defined five functional areas or domains: Manoeuvre Control; Fire Support; Air Defence; Intelligence / Electronic Warfare; and Logistics. As an example, Figure 7.2(b) lists the systems that are fielded, or currently being fielded in the US domains.

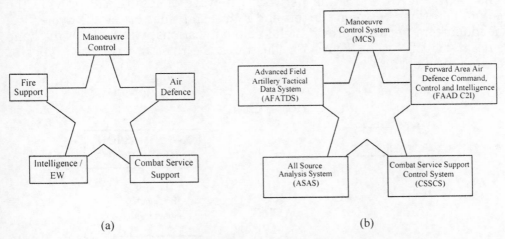

(a)   (b)

Figure 7.2. Battlefield information systems domains.

Generic Architecture

A suitable architecture for a battlefield information system will depend on the size and function of headquarters supported, but Figure 7.3 illustrates a typical generic configuration.

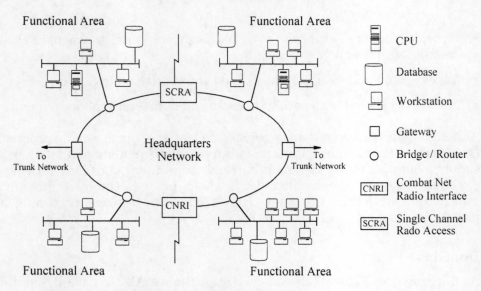

Figure 7.3. Battlefield information systems - generic architecture.

Communications Architecture

The CNRI, SCRA and trunk network gateways of Figure 7.3 provide the communications between the left and right hand sides of the C2 Cycle. The headquarters network provides the communications within the right hand side of the C2 Cycle. Figure 7.4 illustrates the roles of these two types of communications.

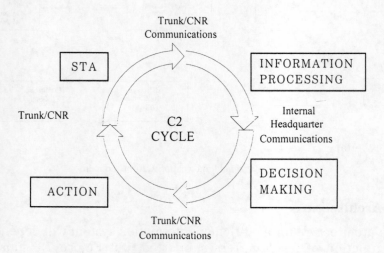

Figure 7.4. Communications Requirements of the C2 Cycle.

Internal Communications

In addition to the external communications required in and out of a headquarters, internal data network communications are required to facilitate information processing and decision making. Functional area networks are normally based on LAN topology such as Ethernet; the headquarters network is based on a MAN technology such as FDDI.

External Communications

The critical communications issue in most external networks is capacity. Modern fibre optic networks within headquarters operate at around 100Mbps, which is currently sufficient to interconnect the functional area LANs that operate at data rates of around 10Mbps. However, a major bottleneck occurs when information is required to be transferred between headquarters across the tactical communications system. The data rates provided by current CNR Sub-systems is 2.4kbps at best for HF and 16kbps for VHF (although information rates on both are considerably lower). The trunk communications sub-system currently provides 16kbps per channel or, if all channels can be aggregated on a trunk link (not always possible), up to 2Mbps is currently possible. To illustrate the inadequacy of the current tactical communications system to cope with interconnection of headquarter networks, Figure 7.5 shows capacity of the various networks as being proportional to physical size.

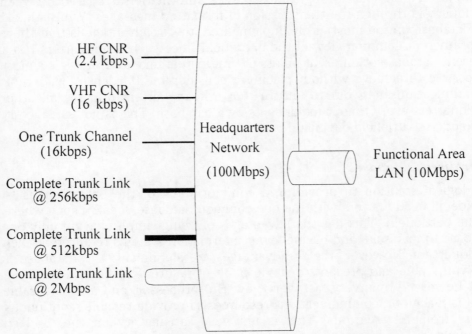

Figure 7.5. Bandwidth comparisons for various battlefield bearers.

Figure 7.5 demonstrates that the battlefield communications system provides a considerable bottleneck and illustrates why the drive in most modern armies is to increase the capacity of trunk links through the use of ATM switching. However, it is unlikely that the data rates available from CNR will significantly increase beyond current levels. Indeed, the current congestion of the HF and VHF spectrum could force a reduction in data rates in some cases.

Database Architecture

One of the key issues for battlefield information systems is the way in which data is stored, processed and distributed. In fact, it could be argued that the design of the database architecture is the fundamental issue for command systems. There are four broad options for the provision of databases to support battlefield information systems - local, centralised, replicated and distributed databases.

Local Databases

In this option, each headquarters holds only the information pertinent to it. In effect, this option simply takes the information from the command post walls and stores it in a database. Whilst the data is most likely to be physically replicated or distributed in a number of places within the headquarters, each headquarter's database is logically separate. Information is shared between headquarters through the transmission of formatted messages. Whilst this is the database option most easily implemented, the disadvantage is that there is no inherent common view of the battlefield since each headquarters has a different database at different points of time. Situational awareness is almost impossible to achieve without placing a considerable burden on the trunk communications network to ensure that a headquarters updates all other headquarters every time it modifies its own database. This is not satisfactory in a modern battlefield command system.

Centralised Databases

The logical solution to providing a common view of the battlefield is to provide all headquarters with the one common database, located somewhere on the battlefield. This has the advantages of being simple, having only one database to maintain, and having fewer information systems required at each headquarters. However, the disadvantages are significant: the database is very vulnerable and presents a single point of failure. The central database must be served by a very fast, very powerful processor, and a considerable drain is placed on communications resources to provide reliable, continuous access from all locations. This is not very satisfactory on the modern battlefield.

Replicated Databases

The first database architecture employed in a major fielded system ensured that the central database was survivable against physical attack and communications outages, by replicating it in a number of locations. One of the copies becomes the 'master' database and the others become 'slaves'. All updates from anywhere on the battlefield are completed on the current master, which ensures that slave databases are updated regularly. If the master database is destroyed or cut-off, one of the slaves becomes the master and the process continues. This technique was employed by the first major battlefield command system, WAVELL, deployed by the British Army in the early to mid 1980s.

A replicated database architecture has the advantages of a centralised database with the additional advantage of survivability. The disadvantages of this technique are the complicated management system and the very high communications overhead required to ensure that all replicated databases are synchronised. This overhead is even higher than for a centralised database, and was the major reason for the failure of WAVELL.

Distributed Databases

The most favoured architecture in modern civilian and military systems is the distributed database architecture, in which data is distributed amongst headquarters with the intention of reducing the communications overheads required to support information transfer. Particular portions of the database are distributed such that the unit that has the most regular need for the data stores that data locally, so as to minimise the amount of access required across the trunk network. For redundancy, data is also replicated, at least locally, although critical information is replicated in a number of locations. Data is normally replicated in at least three locations to accommodate movements of headquarters.

The major advantage of the distributed database architecture is the provision of a common view of the battlefield, with the least drain on sparse trunk and CNR communications. The major disadvantage is the complex management system required. Fortunately, however, such database management systems (DBMS) are now more commonly available in both the civilian and military environments.

Practically, a battlefield system is likely to be a compromise between centralisation, replication and distribution. The major constraining factors of available bandwidth and nodal processing power will most probably dictate the final configuration.

Interoperability

Interoperability is required between command systems within armies, between services and with traditional allies and regional partners. The degree of interoperability must be carefully chosen at the design stage of the command system. Decisions should be based on the necessary, as well as the acceptable, extent of personnel involvement and user access rights.

In its simplest form, two systems may interoperate satisfactorily by the use of a voice circuit. However, real-time, automated information exchange usually requires a higher degree of interoperability. NATO defines five degrees of interoperability between any two battlefield information systems:

- **Degree 1.** The users are separated and can only exchange data using a third system - such as a telephone or teletype link.
- **Degree 2.** The users are able to liaise directly, but the systems are separate.
- **Degree 3.** A single user can operate each system and has a terminal from each system in front of him.
- **Degree 4.** Users of either system are able to communicate directly, but with restrictions on the mutual functions.
- **Degree 5.** The two systems are compatible and interoperate fully.

At present, the best that can be obtained between national systems is Degree 4, although most systems are still only interoperable at Degrees 1, 2 and 3. Normally, data can only be exchanged electronically in pre-determined ways such as through message format.

The issue of interoperability is generally a technical one. Regardless of the ability to interoperate, however, the major issue is sovereignty control. That is, the technical question of whether databases can be accessed by other command systems is normally subordinate to the national security issue of which data is allowed to be shared.

Data Issues

There is a wide variety of information stored within the database of a command system and there are many issues that need to be resolved as part of the system specification and design process. Information management is a key process here, requiring a detailed analysis of the processes that the databases are to support. At the lower level, there are many issues such as who 'owns' the data and therefore has the responsibility to maintain and update it. Data administration and a data dictionary are vital components of managing the command system.

Management Provisions

Management of any large computer network is a demanding task. When the computers are geographically dispersed, linked by multiple communications means, and frequently moved, systems management becomes very complex and poses both a technical and tactical management challenge. Arguably, this management challenge represents the majority of the technical risk associated with the implementation of a battlefield command system.

Technically, the network of information systems must function as a seamless whole. Data flow among computers must not require intensive from the users, who must be free to concentrate on understanding and interpreting the information they receive through the system. *Tactically*, information flow must support the needs of the commander and staff, who should not have to understand the technical processes by which information is made available.

Technical systems management includes:

- planning the network of communications and information systems;
- controlling and monitoring the interconnection of systems and devices;
- maintenance of network performance at the required standard;
- reconfiguring the network as required to accommodate the tactical situation or equipment failures; and
- equipment maintenance.

Tactical systems management ensures information is exchanged and made available to support the tactical plan. Tactical systems management supports the chain of command and includes:

- planning to ensure information availability regardless of changes in the battlefield environment;
- planning database location(s) and replication(s); and
- controlling and monitoring information flow and database transactions.

It should be noted that many of the above tasks coincide with the network management tasks described in Chapter 6 for battlefield communications systems. Practically, the two lists of tasks cannot be separated. Battlefield communications and information systems should be managed as a complete command support system, preferably under the control of the one management structure.

SECURITY

The most important aspect of information system security is the specification of what the security measures are required to achieve. Over-specification leads to very costly systems that users hate to use (and often will not use).

Under-specification can result in the delivery of very expensive systems that are useless. The only fully secure computer is one that has no contact with any operator, and is in a totally secure room that is screened to prevent escaping radiation and has no connections to any other computer or network. Even if such a system were possible, it would unusable. Some compromise must be therefore made.

Traditionally, security can be considered to comprise three elements: *personnel*, *physical* and *electronic* security.

- **Physical Security.** The physical security of the components of a command system is of prime importance. Machines and storage devices containing classified information must be secured in accordance with their classification in a similar manner to classified documents.

- **Personnel Security.** It is essential that the personnel using the computer system can only access data and software for which they hold the appropriate security clearance. Unauthorised access must be prevented and access granted to genuine users in accordance with their clearance. The most likely source of breaches are the human operators, since it is normally much easier and cheaper to corrupt a human than it is to try to break codes etc. Arguably, therefore, the most important security aspect of any computer system is personnel security. The motivation and the loyalty of personnel, particularly those with privileged access to the system, have to be assured throughout the life of the system. Technology can assist in keeping the security risks down to a manageable level, but without the active cooperation of the personnel concerned, any security plan is almost useless.

- **Electronic Security.** Electronic security normally entails measures to improve: software security, access to data, security of data transmission, and prevention of unwanted electromagnetic radiation.

All the security techniques discussed here are complementary. No single technique (such as physical security) can, by itself, effect adequate security. There is a great temptation to rely on technical security measures to provide electronic security and to ignore personnel security measures. This would be ineffective as both operators and engineers are generally able to go around these defences should they so desire. Good computer security is the balanced mix of all security techniques. Since perfect security is very expensive to achieve, an analysis into risk must be undertaken to balance cost versus the risk of compromise.

Modes of Operation

As implied from the discussion above, a computer system will normally be run in one of three security modes:

- *Dedicated Mode* in which all users are fully cleared to access all the data in the system and all users have a need-to-know for all the data;
- *System-High Mode* in which all users are fully cleared to access all the data in the system but do not necessarily have a need-to-know for all the data; or
- *Multi-Level Mode* in which not all the users are cleared to access all the data in the system and usually do not have a need-to-know for all the data.

Dedicated Mode does not require the software to enforce any of the security policy but relies on physical, personnel and procedural security measures. System-High Mode places some trust in the software to enforce the need-to-know principle of electronic security but still relies principally on the other two classes of security measures. Multi-Level Mode entrusts the software to enforce the majority of the security policy but still requires physical security measures to protect the trusted computer base (that is, the computer itself and the associated discs etc).

Radiation Security

The codeword TEMPEST is associated with radiation security, which ensures that any electronic emissions from the system or its communications do not contain information useful to a potential enemy. This is a very specialised area and is currently achieved through good design procedures. Radiation security cannot be added on to a communications or information system; it must be designed in. Radiation security is normally obtained at considerable cost - protected PCs can be approximately 20 times as expensive as commercial PCs. A number of measures can reduce the cost. VDU radiation can be reduced by using plasma displays - giving lower resolution but reduced signature. If there are a number of terminals and computers in the one location such as a shelter, it is often more economical to shield the shelter than to address each terminal and device within it.

Other Issues

Computer security raises a number of difficult peripheral issues:

- software must be as classified as the data it accesses;
- configuration management of classified software is very difficult and expensive - it normally entails more rigorous testing and tighter control than unclassified software;
- security can be considerably enhanced by the implementation of an audit

trail of all operations to identify which information has been compromised by a breach if there is one (at considerable cost and processing overhead);

- multi-level security requires a purpose designed database so that data can be 'tagged' so that its security classification can always be remembered by the system - this is very important in data aggregation to ensure that the result is accorded the classification of the highest classified component; and
- all data transmitted across unsecured line and all radio links should be encrypted.

There are no easy solutions, and we should finish the section as we began it. The most important aspect of information security is to articulate clearly what is to be achieved by the implementation of security measures. The above issues are very difficult to solve and produce a user-friendly system. Potential solutions cannot even begin to eventuate without a clear understanding of the requirement.

SOFTWARE DEVELOPMENT

In recent years, large software-based projects have rarely been delivered on-time, within budget or in accordance with users' expectations. Software is generally unreliable, difficult to transport between systems, and is difficult to maintain and modify. What has been particularly lacking are rigorous design methodologies that can ensure delivery of successful systems. Program testing and debugging takes 50% of the time of a development project. Even so, when it is complete, major software has typically five errors for every hundred program statements. In short, software development techniques are not adequate to cope with current software projects and will reduce in effectiveness as systems continue to grow in complexity.

Software Engineering

This so-called 'software crisis' led to the introduction of *software engineering* which aims to ensure quality software through a disciplined approach to software development. Software engineering provides a controlled development process to develop software with predictable performance through:

- a disciplined approach to software development from concept through to in-service maintenance;
- the establishment of formal methods to provide a disciplined engineering approach to programming;
- the integration of both technical skills (such as design and programming) and non-technical skills (such as project management); and
- the use of computer-based tools to support development and improve productivity.

Central to software engineering is the concept of the *Software Life Cycle* to describe the phases of software development, from initial concept through to in-service maintenance, and to provide a framework for the processes critical to developing quality software.

Traditional Software Life Cycle

As illustrated in Figure 7.6, the Waterfall Model provides a sequential development procedure where each phase is to be completed before moving on to the next. The output of each phase is normally a number of deliverables in the form of documentation or software, which are used as the input to the next phase. Software project management and project control are achieved by setting milestones against the intermediate and final deliverables of each phase. Contractor payment is normally linked to milestones and deliverables as a mechanism for maintaining cost and schedule constraints.

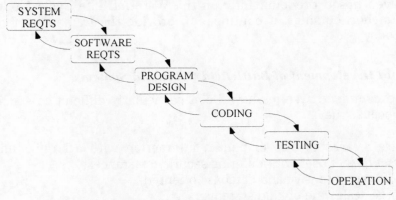

Figure 7.6. The Waterfall Model

Whilst the Waterfall Model has proved useful for the development of many systems, it has a number of shortcomings. It assumes that it is possible with a small amount of initial investment to write a complete specification for the system; and that, once established, the requirements will remain unaltered during the development of the project.

The principal prerequisite of the strategy is a complete, correct and unambiguous specification of requirements. This has proved to be almost impossible to achieve since it is unlikely that the full use of the system can be anticipated at such an early stage as users often do not know what they want the system to do. An automated system provides many advances over a manual system; so many that they can rarely be specified completely in advance.

Therefore, more often than not, the original specification must be modified as the user becomes more familiar with the requirements and with the potential offered by an automated system. However, change destabilises the Waterfall Model as there are no inherent project management procedures available to track changes across software components and specifications.

Another major flaw with the traditional procurement strategy is that it ignores rapid change in technology and strategic guidance. Requirements are frozen at the outset of the project, which leads 10 to 15 years later to the introduction into service of systems that are already obsolete. Additionally, since requirements specifications are not validated until the end of the project when the system has been built, any errors are difficult and expensive, if not impossible, to remedy. In fact, on average, software maintenance accounts for up to 80% of life cycle costs but is rarely budgeted for when project costs are estimated.

Despite these shortcomings, development standards such as MIL-STD-2167A have evolved based predominantly on the Waterfall Life Cycle Model and, despite its short-comings, it continues to provide the framework for many projects today.

Traditional Development of Battlefield Command Systems

Battlefield command systems have been particularly difficult to specify and develop because they:

- require a large degree of human interaction with a large number of diversetypes of user with differing security clearances;
- are software intensive and database oriented;
- are large scale, one-of-kind systems;
- are normally based on a heterogeneous mix of multi-processor and distributed processor environment including embedded computers;
- have a long lifetime (10 to 20 years) due to cost and procurement constraints;
- are based on imprecise requirements that are continually changing to provide enhancements that keep pace with changes in the modern battlefield;
- have a complex upgrade process due to the need to maintain a current operational capability across the army and with allies; and
- require extensive maintenance due to their complex nature.

Traditional Software Development and the Materiel Cycle

The major difficulty is that members of the software development community cannot find a solution to the issues mentioned earlier. Their approach to the failure of software projects has been to insist on more time spent specifying requirements up front and to minimise changes to the system. Unfortunately both of these measures lead to systems that take even longer to introduce into service and are even less useful when the user finally sees the product of his initial thoughts from 5 to 10 years ago.

The difficulties with the traditional life cycle are exacerbated by the traditional military materiel procurement cycles, in particular:

- long lead times of 5 to 10 years in capability development due to the long committee-based processes and difficulty in establishing precise requirements;
- long times to contract since the contract must be based on a complete statement of specifications;
- unwieldy contract management since contract milestones are based on delivery of a large number of documents, the approval of which takes considerable time and often causes considerable delay;
- the lack of user access during the development process, which is made worse by contracting processes that prohibit major changes without going through the development process once more; and
- a marked distinction between the *Introduction into Service* and the *Maintenance* phases of the development cycle, which is based on the expectation that a complete system is introduced into service and only upgraded by an abbreviated version of the procurement cycle.

A new software development methodology is required for developing software-intensive command systems. It must not ignore the dynamic nature of the requirements and must allow for advances in technology and evolving user perceptions and refinements of their needs. Users must be provided with early capabilities so that requirements can be evolved over the subsequent phases of development so that the system will be able to reach its full potential.

Evolutionary Acquisition

Unlike the traditional procurement procedures, *evolutionary acquisition (EA)* does not demand that requirements are specified completely up front. Rather, specification can occur incrementally throughout the project, as the requirements become clearer to the developer and user. Systems delivered to date using EA have had a high success rate in achieving user satisfaction and meeting budget and time scale constraints.

EA is a procurement strategy for acquiring systems in an incremental fashion. The only initial activities that are necessary are the specification of the overall system requirements, in sufficient detail to allow the assessment of technological and financial implications; and a detailed system architecture that can accommodate flexibility of requirements.

The process begins with a first iteration of the system that consists of a set of clearly defined capabilities that can be quickly implemented. This allows the users to gain experience of the technology and to refine requirements for subsequent iterations. The project consists of a series of well-planned iterations, each adding to the capabilities of the system. The process provides sufficient latitude to allow the implementation of capabilities resulting from altering requirements and advances in technology. The complete system is built using this 'build a little, test a little, field a little' philosophy. From a management point of view, managing and budgeting, each iteration can be treated as a discrete, stand-alone package, which can be bounded and funded. This simplifies the management of monitoring and controlling the project.

A Life Cycle Model for Evolutionary Acquisition

A Life Cycle Model is an important necessity because it defines how a project will be managed. The success or failure of a project may hang on the choice of Life Cycle Model. Boehm's Spiral Model has become synonymous with EA, however, use of the Spiral Model is not exclusive to any particular procurement strategy.

The Spiral Model is compatible with EA and overcomes the difficulties encountered by the Waterfall Model by focusing on risk rather than deliverables.

The Spiral Model does not mandate that requirements are specified completely in advance. Rather, a manageable, well-defined set of requirements is developed based on a Reference Architecture that comprises an Operational Architecture, a Technical Architecture and a Systems Architecture. An early prototype is developed to elicit comments from users and to assist in the dialogue between users and developers. Once the first package of work is complete, it is reviewed in a process that allows users, developers and project managers to evaluate the product and to prepare a plan for the next stage of development.

CONCLUSION

That completes our brief consideration of battlefield information systems and, for that matter, of all of the technologies associated with battlefield command systems. It has not been possible to do more than skate over the fundamentals of the communications and information systems that underpin battlefield command systems. However, the book is intended to be an introduction and cannot hope to cover each of the topics in the depth that it deserves. Hopefully, though, the reader's understanding has been increased in this critical area.

Appendix I
Basic Circuit Theory

This appendix briefly introduces the concept of current, voltage and power and the circuit components of resistance, capacitance and inductance.

VOLTAGE, CURRENT AND RESISTANCE

As illustrated in Figure I-1(a), if the positive and negative terminals of a *voltage* source (a battery, for example) are connected, then electrons will be attracted to the positive terminal. These electrons will be supplied from the negative terminal and will flow through the connecting wire. Since the flow of electrons is a little microscopic for us to worry about, we normally consider the average flow rate of electrons, that is the number of electrons per second. We call this flow *current*, and measure it in Amperes, or Amps (A). The flow of current is represented in Figure I-1(b).

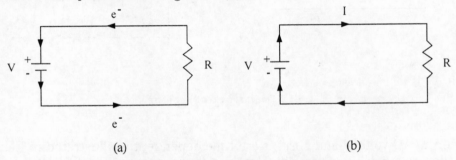

(a)   (b)

Figure I-1. Voltage, current and resistance.

Now, the number of electrons that will flow will depend on the degree of freedom of electrons in the conducting wire. The ability of the wire to conduct is called *conductance*, but this property of the wire is normally considered in terms of how it restricts the flow of electrons, that is its *resistance*. Resistance is measured in Ohms (Ω).

Since the *current* results from the electrons supplied by the *voltage* source and the *resistance* is the reluctance of the wire to allow the electrons to move through it, it makes sense for these three properties to be related. They are, by Ohm's Law:

$$V = IR$$

Direct and Alternating Current

When the voltage is supplied by a constant source such as the battery in Figure I-1, the current supplied is constant and is called *direct current (DC)*. Figure I-2(a) shows that the current (I) is constant over time. This makes sense since, from Ohm's Law, the resistance (R) is constant for a given wire, so that a constant voltage (V) must produce a constant current.

When the voltage source varies in value with time, the resistance remains constant so that the current must also vary in proportion with the voltage. The most common varying current is *alternating current (AC)*, which varies sinusoidally with time, as shown in Figure I-2(b).

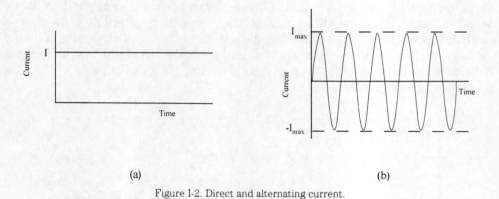

(a)   (b)

Figure I-2. Direct and alternating current.

Since the AC voltage and current are time-dependent as illustrated in Figure I-3, their relationship is described by the time-variant version of Ohm's Law:

$$v(t)=i(t)\ R$$

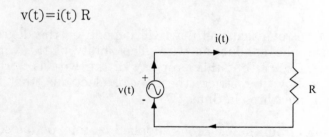

Figure I-3. Voltage, current and resistance.

Average and RMS Voltage and Current

As illustrated in Figure I-4(a), the average value of an alternating current is also zero. This means that the average voltage is zero.

$$I_{av} = 0 = V_{av}$$

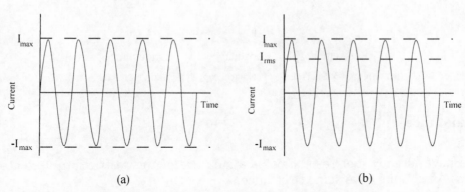

(a)   (b)

Figure I-4. Maximum and RMS current.

Yet the alternating voltage and current have an effect over time, which does not seem to make sense if they have an average value of zero. So, a current, I_{rms}, (the root mean square current) is defined as the DC current that has the same effect as the AC current i(t).We do not want to get into the maths here, but it can be shown after some calculus that:

$$I_{rms} = \frac{I_{max}}{\sqrt{2}} \quad \text{and} \quad V_{rms} = \frac{V_{max}}{\sqrt{2}}$$

POWER

When the flow of electrons is slowed by a resistance, they must give up some of their energy. The dissipation of energy over time is called *power (P)*. The power dissipated in a resistance, R, is given by:

$$P = VI$$

Since V=IR, the equation can also be written: $P = I^2R$ or $P = \frac{V^2}{R}$

For AC currents, the power dissipated in a resistance is calculated in terms of the root mean square values. That is:

$$P = I_{rms}^2 R = \frac{I_{max}^2}{2} R \quad \text{or} \quad P = \frac{V_{rms}^2}{R} = \frac{V_{max}^2}{2R}$$

CIRCUIT COMPONENTS

Figure I-5 shows the symbols for the circuit components of resistance, capacitance and inductance.

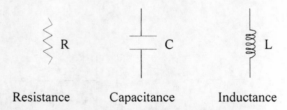

Resistance   Capacitance   Inductance

Figure I-5. Symbols for resistance, capacitance and inductance.

Resistance

We have already met resistance as a measure of the restriction of electron flow. All circuits have some resistance.

Capacitance

The capacitor is obtained by placing two conducting plates near to each other, separated by a non-conducting material called a dielectric. The capacitance, C, of the capacitor is measured in Farad (F). A voltage across the plates results in an electric field between them and the current that flows is directly proportional to the time rate of change of the voltage across the plates. A capacitor therefore acts as an open circuit to DC.

Inductance

A current passing through a wire will produce a magnetic field around the wire. Winding the conductor into a coil strengthens the magnetic field. The resulting element is called an inductor, whose inductance (L) is measured in the Henry (H). The voltage across an inductor is directly proportional to the time rate of change of the current through it. An inductor therefore acts as a short circuit to DC.

Appendix II
Decibels

Early telephone engineers discovered that the human ear did not respond to changes on a linear scale. A linear scale would suggest that if you doubled the output power of a speaker, the sound would be twice as large. In fact, the sound would be only slightly louder since the relationship is logarithmic and it would take ten times the input power to double the volume. This logarithmic ratio was called the *Bel*, because the engineers worked for the Bell Telepohone Company.

$$Bel = \log_{10}\left(\frac{P_2}{P_1}\right)$$ where P_1 and P_2 are the powers being compared

Because the Bel is a fairly small unit of measurement, and produces fractions, the *decibel* is normally used. The decibel (dB) is ten times the Bel.

$$dB = 10\log\left(\frac{P_2}{P_1}\right)$$

If a system has an input of 2 W and an output of 6 W, the output is three times larger and the gain of the system is said to be 3. In dB, the gain is:

$$Gain = 10\log\left(\frac{6}{2}\right) = 4.77 \text{ dB}$$

Now, a system can also have a smaller output than the input, which is called a loss or a negative gain. For example, if the system we used earlier had an input of 6 W and an output of 2 W, then its gain would be:

$$Gain = 10\log\left(\frac{2}{6}\right) = -4.77 \text{ dB}$$

Therefore, the system has a -4.77 dB gain or, more commonly we say, a 4.77 dB loss.

dBm and dBW

The decibel can also be used to express a power level, provided a reference or zero-dB level is known. In other words, a certain power (P_1) is expressed as a ratio with a particular reference level of power P_R such that:

$$dB = 10 \log (P_1/P_R)$$

There are two standard types: dBW and dBm.

DBW

One standard power level reference is 1W or 0dBW, since:

$$0dBW = 10 \log (1W/1W)$$

The capital "W" in dBW means that the power is in reference to 1 Watt. For example, a 5 W transmitter can also be said to have an output of:

$$10 \log (5/1) = 6.98 \text{ dBW}$$

DBM

Often the powers we are talking about are quite small, such as in the powers received in communications systems. A more appropriate standard reference is 1mW or 0dBm, since:

$$0dBm = 10 \log(1mW/1mW)$$

The "m" on the end of dBm means that the power is in reference to 1 mW.

Voltage Ratios in Decibels

Voltage ratios can also be expressed in decibels by noting that:

$$\text{power ratio} = 10\log\frac{P_2}{P_1} \text{ and } P_2 = \frac{V_2^2}{R}, \quad P_1 = \frac{V_1^2}{R}$$

so that

$$\text{power ratio} = 10\log\frac{V_2^2}{V_1^2} = 10\log\left(\frac{V_2}{V_1}\right)^2 = 20\log\frac{V_2}{V_1}$$

Index